To Flossie

Printed in the United States of America
ISBN 0-931011-40-X

First Printing – November, 1992

An Easy Course in Using DOS

by Chet Langin

Illustrated by Virginia Rohrbacher

Grapevine Publications, Inc.

P.O. Box 2449

Corvallis, Oregon 97339-2449 U.S.A.

Contents

What's in This Book?

This book *teaches* you DOS. The idea here is to *understand*—not just to memorize. Sure, you'll find everything here from **AUTOEXEC.BAT** to **CTRL**-**Z**. In fact, you'll see and learn over 50 DOS commands. Some are fabulous; others are frivolous—but that's the point of this book: To help you separate the useful from the useless.

Maybe you want to "learn it all." Maybe you're looking to learn just a few vital commands—just enough so that you can use a computer to get your own work done. Maybe you just want to get the big picture, to educate yourself and simply become "computer literate."

Well, you can do all those things here in this book. There will be points along the way to guide you toward each of these goals.

What's Not in This Book?

Since this is a book dedicated to *teaching*—not just to *documenting*—you won't find every last DOS command covered here. Some are just too specialized to be of much general interest or value.

So if you're looking for explanations of **CTTY, SHARE, LINK, EXE2BIN, ASSIGN, JOIN, SUBST**, the **GWBASIC*** commands, or most of the assembly language* commands, read your manuals.

---

*To learn to program well in BASIC or in assembly language would require an entire book, anyway.

How You Should Use This Book

Many people skim or skip through computer books. Often this is because the books are meant to be used that way—more as references than as readable tutorials.

This Easy Course is different. It's a conversational narrative—like that of a teacher in a classroom. It covers first things first—and then builds upon them, offering examples and explanations at every step.

So *don't skip around* except at the designated "skip points." You'll be missing too much good stuff if you do:

Part I   **Understanding the Computer** (Chapters 1-3): How the computer developed. Hardware, software, how they work. The idea of an operating system. Key concepts in DOS.

Part II   **Getting Up To Speed** (Chapters 4-6): How to install DOS on your computer. What the computer does when you turn it on. Recognizing the DOS prompt and the DOS Shell.

Part III **Using DOS** (Chapters 7-11): How to make, save, copy, and print files. How to manage your files with a disk tree. How to back up files. Mousing around in the DOS Shell.

Part IV   **Mastering DOS** (Chapters 12-15): How to save work with batch files. How to customize your computer. Taking a microscopic view of files—the individual bytes. A little bit of assembly language programming. What to study next.

1. CREATING THE COMPUTER

Manual Counting Machines

From the beginning of history, people have had at least one basic problem: how to do all the counting, calculating, and recordkeeping necessary for civilization.

Indeed, how *do* you count sheep ... tally up crops ... take a census ... do business with a profit ... send spaceships to the moon? As civilization got more complicated, this problem did, too.

The modern computer is the result of efforts to solve this problem.*

Mind you, this solution wasn't invented overnight—or even over a hundred years. It goes back all the way to Adam and Eve, for they had in their hands the first human computing devices—fingers.

Of course, there are still lots of calculating tricks you can do with your fingers,** but they're definitely limited when it comes to computations of any length or complexity.

So a number of mechanical inventions were created to overcome those limitations....

*If you're not interested in learning how the computer was developed—and you want to miss a really fascinating tale—then go ahead and skip over to page 40.

**Many of these are still used by desperate students everywhere.

Abacus

Developed in Asia, this ancient instrument has beads which can be moved back and forth on rods. If a bead is pushed towards the central bar, it is counted; otherwise, it isn't. A bead may have a value of 1, 5, 10, 50, and so forth, *depending upon its location.*

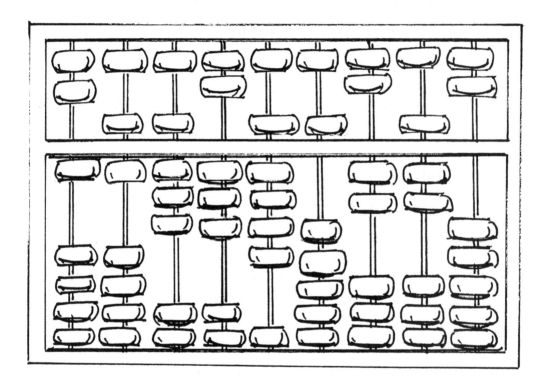

Because of its ability to represent different *place values,* the abacus is actually quite efficient and is still in use in parts of the world, primarily Asia. In fact, there's a story told about when electronic calculators were first being introduced in Japan: An experienced abacus user challenged a calculator salesman to a speed contest—and won!

Quipu

The Incas in 15th-Century Peru didn't have a written language. So they needed some way not only to add and count but to _record_ the result, also.

Their solution? Knotted ropes, called _quipus_ (pronounced "key-poos").

Imagine holding a single rope with one end in each hand. Now, imagine additional ropes tied to the first one so that they hang loose (like the beginning of a macrame).

Each hanging rope represented something: The number of people in a village; the number of items in a storage area; ...you name it.

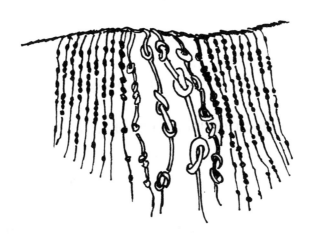

Knots were tied on the hanging ropes to indicate amounts. The position of a knot on a rope determined its value—so this was another way to represent place-value. And of course, the knots representing values could be added and subtracted, and the result stayed securely knotted in the quipu until changed purposely.

Place Values in Decimal Numbers

The abacus gave special importance to the location of a bead. The quipu gave special importance to the location of a knot. But this idea of *place value* was most fully realized by Arab mathematicians, who developed the symbolic arithmetic system—with *decimal numerals* and the idea of place value—that is so widely used today. It was an *enormous* advance in computation.

Consider what you would need to do simply to write down the number 50—*without* using place value:

You could simply use 50 of the same "counting" symbol...

|||||||||||||||||||||||||||||||||||||||||||||||||||

...but—just at a glance—is that 50 or 51?

You could still use one basic symbol, but also a little *grouping:*

||||| ||||| ||||| ||||| ||||| ||||| ||||| ||||| ||||| |||||

or

JHT JHT JHT JHT JHT JHT JHT JHT JHT JHT

But those groups start to look like symbols of their own, no? So you could take that idea one step further:

5 5 5 5 5 5 5 5 5 5

Or, you could simply invent one unique symbol to mean "fifty:" §

But what about numbers such as 1,675,011, 3.1416, 99.44—or 0?

Can you imagine trying to calculate molecular weights, orbital trajectories or national debts without a place-value numbering system?

Neither could those Arab mathematicians. They found that for larger numbers, it was much easier to use grouping *and* unique symbols—to let each symbol's place *within* the group denote its value:

If a *5* is in the "ones," place (*5*), it stands for the value *five*.
If the *5* is in the "tens" place (*50*), it stands for the value *fifty*.

The *place* of the *5* determines its *value*, hence the name, *place value*.

Notice the immense importance of the symbol, *0*: It's a *place holder,* so that, even if the number 50 has no "ones," you'll still know that the 5 is in the *"tens"* place.

Well, this simple system lets you write down *enormous* numbers using very few symbols (*0-9*)—and do arithmetic quickly and reliably, too.

It's so obvious—and so easy—you don't even think about it, but it's one of the greatest inventions of mankind. It spread into Europe from Arabia in the 12th Century. This is why—thanks to symbolic "place values"—the most widely used calculator in the world today is still...

...pencil and paper.

Mechanical Calculators

There are inconveniences to pencil and paper, too, though.

Have you ever shopped for groceries on a tight budget? Maybe you took along a calculator to keep a running total of the cost of the items in your cart—so you'd know quickly when you had reached your limit.

Yes, it's a nuisance to try to shop and do pencil-and-paper calculations simultaneously. But just a few years ago, electronic calculators were not available. The best thing around at the time was a handheld mechanical adding machine—something like a car odometer.

This device had four small wheels with the digits *0 - 9* printed around each wheel. You entered a number by setting the values of the wheels. If a wheel went past the digit *9*, it would advance the next wheel by one digit. Then you would enter the next value, and the next, etc. The nifty device would keep track of your current total.

Schickard

Leonardo da Vinci (1452-1519) wrote about such a device, but it was in 1623 that German-born Wilhelm Schickard actually made one.

His version was considerably larger than the later shopper's version, but since in those days an enormous amount of effort was spent by armies of accountants doing all their calculations by hand, Schickard's device still had great potential. Unfortunately it was destroyed in a fire, so the accountants never got a chance to use it.

Pascal

After another 20 years or so (in 1642) one of those accountants finally got fed up with the tedium of repetitious hand calculations. So he up and created a mechanical calculator.

This "accountant" was actually the French mathematician Blaise Pascal, who was doing some accounting for his father. Seeing the opportunity and potential, Pascal went on to make different models of his calculator—sized to fit on desks—similar in size to today's cash registers.

So although the logic and mechanics of it were established long before his time, Pascal is usually given credit for inventing the mechanical calculator, because he finally produced working devices that served many practical uses. And some of these originals still exist!

Leibniz

After Pascal, inventors sought to create calculators to solve all sorts of problems, not just addition. German mathematician Gottfried Leibniz—best known for his contributions to calculus—created a mechanical calculator in 1673 which also multiplied and divided.

But Leibniz made another contribution which was eventually to play a major role in the development of the computer. He formally described the binary numerical system—the system that uses only *1*'s and *0*'s— to represent numbers and math. Today's computers use this binary system to do *everything they do.*

The Jacquard Loom

A major event in the development of computers had nothing to do with numbers. It had to do with weaving.

That's right—weaving. In order to make a pattern when working a loom, the operators had to choose and use the proper colors of thread for each row of the cloth. This was mindless, tedious job for the operators, as they worked from preset patterns. It was a pain.

The tedium was not lost on a young French mill worker named Joseph Jacquard. In 1801, he succeeded in building a better loom—a system based on *punched cards:*

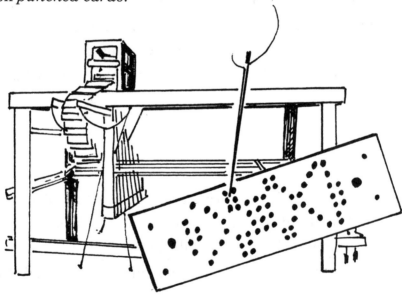

Needles were aimed at the cards. If the needles encountered holes in the cards, they went through, resulting in certain colors of thread being chosen. Voila! By punching holes in the cards in certain places, the designer could guarantee what pattern the needles produced! The Jacquard Loom was so successful that thousands were made.

Babbage's Analytical Engine

Inventor Charles Babbage (1792-1871) of England borrowed the idea of punched cards to design a mechanical device called the Analytical Engine—which was to have been the first general-purpose calculator.

Babbage's engine was divided into three parts.

1. The *mill*, where the actual calculating was done, used shafts containing computing wheels with the last shaft connected by gears to the first one. Thus, any resulting *output* could be sent back as *input*. This allowed it to accomplish repeated, cumulative additions and subtractions (i.e. multiplication and division).

2. The *store* was comparable to a modern computer's memory. It was where information needed in future calculations, such as intermediate results, were kept.

3. *Punched cards*, like those of Jacquard's Loom, controlled the machine. Some cards contained instructions; others held data.

So nearly 150 years ago, somebody had at least conceived of a machine with the same basic components as the modern computer—a *processor* (his mill), a *memory* (his store) and *programming* (his punched cards).

Unfortunately, Babbage's Analytical Engine was never actually completed, because of the expense and the technology required to make the machine's intricate parts.

Hollerith and the U.S. Census

Meanwhile—while still not true computers—mechanical adding machines were nevertheless helping accountants immensely. But there was one particularly vast and complex counting job they just couldn't handle—the U.S. Census. To collect all the various data was a hard enough task, but then to compile and count it was a nightmare.

Well, Herman Hollerith was in charge of the 1890 census, and he wasn't looking forward to the prospect. So he set out to make it easier. What he did was to combine techniques from Pascal's calculator and Jacquard's (and Babbage's) punched cards.

Census data was stored on these punched cards. Each hole-position in the card represented something (i.e. the cards used a form of _place value_). For example a given position could mean "male" if a hole was punched there, but "female" if it was unpunched.

A "keypunch" machine was devised to actually punch the holes as triggered by an operator, who read the raw data and pressed certain keys on a keyboard. Then a second machine read the cards, keeping a running count of the holes on a series of dials. Electricity was used to detect the holes, but the machine was still essentially mechanical.

Hollerith's machine was so productive that he was soon able to start a business—the Tabulating Machine Company, which merged with others to become the Computing-Tabulating-Recording Company. Later, it was renamed again: International Business Machines Corp.

Perhaps you've heard of it.

Electrifying the Calculating Machine

As electricity became popular in the early part of this century, some people realized that logic was essential for its use.

Consider, for example, a stairwell light controlled by two wall switches—one at the top of stairs and one at the bottom. You've probably seen this: The wiring must be such that if either switch is changed, the status of the light will also change.

That solution required the use of *logical* wiring. But if logical wiring can do something as convenient as control a lighting scheme in a house, could it not also be used to control computations—like an electrical version of Jacquard's punched cards?

*Perhaps—**IF**...*

1.   The *logic* could be developed properly...

2.   The *calculations* could be done *as fast as the electrical instructions*...

3.   The instructions somehow could be *stored* by electricity.

Though the *concept* was well understood, these were the big "if's"—the tough *practical* problems to be solved before the first modern (electrical) computer could be built.

The Logic Problem

The logic problem had already been solved nearly a century earlier—but nobody could foresee its practical implications then.

In 1854, Englishman George Boole published a theory on how logic could be represented by symbols. He found that logical statements could be represented in two quantities: _1_ and _0_. If a statement was true, it was represented by _1_; if false, by _0_. Thus, where Leibniz had previously used _1_'s and _0_'s for math, Boole now used them for logic.

Boole described a set of _operators_ to be used by this two-based (_binary_) logic, to make more complex statements from simpler ones.

Example: Look at the following sentence:

If Bill gets the highest score on the test or Bill scores a 90% on the test, then he will receive an "A" grade for the test.

Boole would see three simpler statements within this.
Statement A: _Bill gets the highest score on the test._
Statement B: _Bill gets a 90% score on the test._
Statement C: _Bill receives an "A" grade on the test._

Boole would then simplify the sentence into:

_If A_ **OR** _B, then C_

As an operator, **OR** means that C is true if either A or B is true.

1. Creating the Computer

When 1's and 0's are assigned to represent true and false, Boole's logic shows that:

0 **OR** 0 = 0   (Both A and B are false, so C is false);
1 **OR** 0 = 1   (A is true and B is false, so C is true);
0 **OR** 1 = 1   (A is false, but B is true, so C is true);
1 **OR** 1 = 1   (Both A and B are true, so C is true).

Bill gets his "A" if he meets at least one (not necessarily both) of the requirements. This is **OR** logic.

But it wasn't until 1938 that the potential of this "Boolean Algebra" was fully recognized. In that year, American-born Claude Shannon published a paper showing how Boole's logical operators could be applied to computers.

Shannon showed how Boolean Algebra could also be used for doing Leibniz's binary math—addition, subtraction, multiplication, and division of binary numbers! *You can create these four binary math operations from various combinations of Boole's logic operators!*

Not only that, binary numbers, with only *two* values (*0* and *1*) was perfectly suited for electricity: A current of electricity (on = true) is represented by *1*; and the lack of a current (off = false) by *0*.

Once this connection was made between Boolean Algebra, binary math, and electricity, the computer revolution was set to begin!

Here's how the logic all got put together:

Each tiny electrical circuit in a computer can be either on or off (*1* or *0*). So each circuit carries one **bit** ("**bi**nary dig**it**") of information. A bit is only enough information to tell the computer to make a simple choice between two options—"go left" or "go right," "do this" or "skip it," etc. But that's not much information—not even enough to hold a number bigger than *1*!

Therefore, these circuits (bits) are organized into *groups* which can carry larger chunks of meaning. The most common of these groups is a group of eight bits, called a **byte**.*

With its 8 bits, a byte can represent a reasonable amount of information. For example, it can represent any number from 0 to 255:

00000000 = 0	01111110 = 126	11111100 = 252
00000001 = 1	01111111 = 127	11111101 = 253
00000010 = 2	10000000 = 128	11111110 = 254
00000011 = 3	10000001 = 129	11111111 = 255
...	...	

After 255, you run out of combinations. So there are 256 ways (0-255) that you can arrange the 8 bits in a byte.**

*Computer humor: Half of a byte (four bits) is called a **nibble**. (Really!)

**If you tend to confuse the names *bit* and *byte*, just remember that the names match the sizes: The word "bit" is smaller than the word "byte"—and a bit is indeed smaller than a byte.

A byte is also enough information to represent the alphabet. This works like those secret agent decoder rings in the cereal boxes—with a simple substitution code:*

$01000001 = A$	$01001110 = N$	$01100001 = a$
$01000010 = B$	$01001111 = O$	$01100010 = b$
$01000011 = C$	$01010000 = P$	$01100011 = c$
$01000100 = D$	$01010001 = Q$	$01100100 = d$
...	...	...

Notice that the difference between upper case and lower case letters is simply a single bit (the third from the left).

Question: How does the computer know if a byte, say 01000010, refers to the letter B or to the number 66?

Answer: The computer doesn't *know* anything. Does a hammer know whether it's driving a nail or cracking walnuts? Of course not. Likewise, a computer doesn't know if a byte is a character or a number. Like the hammer, the computer is a *tool* that merely follows instructions (given to it by humans): Print the byte, display it, add it, store it, etc. It is a human being that interprets that byte to mean what he/she wants it to mean.

---

*This special code is called the American Standard Code for Information Interchange (**ASCII**) code. It's pronounced "as-key."

The Speed Problem

Logic was probably the easiest part of the challenge faced by early computer designers. The really hard part was designing electrical circuits that could handle Boolean logic and carry enough information quickly enough to be practical.

But there were incentives: During World War II, the country needed computers, and needed them quickly—for weapons systems—and so large amounts of time and money were spent creating them.

Howard Aiken of Harvard University and Thomas Watson of IBM cooperated in 1944 in the creation of an electro-mechanical computer called the **Mark I**. It was called "electro-mechanical" because it used *relays*—electrical switches which physically closed and opened to turn the currents on and off.*

These relays, however, took too much time to operate to be practical. What these first-generation computers needed were electrical switches that could close and open more nearly at the speed of electricity—not at the speed of your average mousetrap. This was a problem that would not be solved right away.

---

*This made the Mark I sound somewhat like a roomful of workers knitting frantically with steel needles (Joseph Jacquard would have been proud).

The Storage Problem

Speedy or not, computers also needed a way to use electricity to *store* the status of bits. When an interim solution to a problem was reached, a computer would need to store this information until it was needed in a future calculation.

Ever since Schickard's time (1623) this storage had been done mechanically with dials. But again, the problem was that the speed of the storage needed to match the speed of the processing—i.e. you had to do it electrically. That's no easy task: How do you store something in a moving, ephemeral thing like an electrical current?

In 1939, John Atanasoff, a professor at Iowa State, figured out how to do it all with **vacuum tubes**. These vacuum tubes could be used to store electrical circuits and also control the logical processing of them! And the tubes didn't physically move—no more mousetrap relays. This is why Atanasoff is often referred to as the inventor or Father of the Computer.

Another researcher of the period, John Mauchly, had set out to create a computer during the war, to help speed up calculations of bombing trajectories. He visited Atanasoff and saw how the vacuum tubes were used in Atanasoff's computer. Then, while Atanasoff joined the Navy (and missed out on developing his vacuum tube idea further), Mauchly went on to build the **E**lectronic **N**umerical **I**ntegrator **A**nd **C**alculator (**ENIAC**) in 1946.

The **ENIAC**, with its vacuum tubes, became the first all-electronic general-purpose computer that could *store data*.

New Problems: Size, Cost, Heat, Reliability

The Mark I, ENIAC, and other prototype computers were all gargantuan machines that occupied entire rooms. They were designed principally to help solve big problems of the time: Calculating trajectories and other information for weapon systems.

But they created new problems:

- They were huge—and extremely expensive.

- They used vast amounts of electricity. All by itself, ENIAC used 140,000 watts—the total output of a small power station.

- They created too much heat. Massive, complicated cooling systems were devised to keep the components from short-circuiting and catching fire.

- The vacuum tubes were too delicate. Initially, one of the 18,000 tubes in ENIAC would fail every 15 minutes.

Using the technological momentum of the end of World War II, technicians sought to correct these new problems.

Making a More Powerful Computer

Decreasing the Size

These days a small personal computer has more computational power than the original giant computers. How is this possible? The answer lies in the "shrinking" of the bit—decreasing the amount of space needed for a controllable electrical circuit.

The first step in downscaling computers was the ***transistor***. It was invented in the 1940's, but was not used in computers until the late 1950's.

Transistors are made of solid material instead of gases or liquids (that is, they are "solid state"). Like vacuum tubes, transistors can store bits—the "off/on" states of currents of electricity. But they're much smaller than vacuum tubes, last longer, use less energy, and—best of all—they are much faster. So as a bit-storage method, transistors were a much better match for the fast electrical operations the computer would do on those bits.

Computers shrank again with the ***integrated circuit*** (**IC**) or, more informally, the "computer chip."

The chip is a *group* of transistors and other electronic components which are miniaturized and constructed as a unit. The first chips were used in computers in the late 1960's. The equivalent of thousands of vacuum tubes can be put on a single chip(!).

Large Scale Integration (**LSI**) was the next advancement for computers. This name is just techno-lingo for "the chips got smaller."*

Three types of LSI chips emerged:

1. A **C**entral **P**rocessing **U**nit (**CPU**) is the collection of computational and controlling functions (the "control center") of a computer—all put onto a single chip. Remember how Babbage's analytical engine had a mill and a store? The mill was where the work was done and the store was where the information was kept. In modern computers, the CPU is the mill where the work is done.

2. **R**andom **A**ccess **M**emory (**RAM**) chips contain temporary storage areas that function as long as the machine is turned on. They are the equivalent of Babbage's store area: RAM is the storage area for the bits that the CPU processes. The processing may change the states of any of these bits.

3. A **R**ead **O**nly **M**emory (**ROM**) chip is also a memory unit—like RAM—except that its memory (the states of its bits) cannot be changed by the CPU. Also, ROM memory isn't erased when the machine is turned off; it is *non-volatile*.

So the creation of these integrated chips meant that engineers could use them together in a relatively small space to make a relatively small computer—a personal-sized computer!

---

*But the "shrinking" continued ... Next came VLSI chips (Very Large Scale Integration)—i.e. "Very Small Chips." What used to require several computer chips can now be fitted onto just one. And the shrinking continues to this day...

Improving the Memory of Computers

The size reduction of chips had enormous benefits for RAM and ROM—obviously: *More memory fits into less space.* Early personal computers typically had 64K* of RAM. Today, 640K is standard, and even higher amounts are becoming common.

But there have been other improvements in computer memory, too. When a computer is first turned on, it obtains its *first* instructions from a ROM chip built into the computer. And some of those instructions tell it to conduct a self-test, to be sure that every single bit of RAM is working properly.

And problems are relatively rare now, too. Remember the old television sets with the vacuum tubes? Every now and then a tube would blow and require replacement. Newer TV's are solid state—much more reliable—and so is modern computer memory.

*"K" normally stands for the prefix, *kilo-*, meaning "1000." However, when used in reference to computers, "K" stands for 1,024, because of the binary numerical system which computers use:

Binary		= Decimal	
1		1	
10		2	
100		4	
1000		8	
10000		16	
100000		32	
1000000		64	Thus 64K = 64 x 1,024 = 65,536 bytes
10000000		128	
100000000		256	and
1000000000		512	
10000000000		1,024	640K = 640 x 1,024 = 655,360 bytes

Remember, 64K refers to *bytes.* 64K = 65,536 bytes = 524,288 bits. And 640K = 5,242,880 bits. Today's personal computers have over *5 million bits* of memory!

Increasing the Speed of Computers

Integrated circuits and computer chips weren't just smaller; they also solved the other problems of the giant mainframes: They used much less electricity. They created much less heat. The chips were more durable than vacuum tubes and were cheaper to produce.

The size factor alone made the computers faster. After all, if your circuit is smaller, it simply takes less time for the current to travel around it—i.e. to "flip the bit" from *0* to *1*. But scientists also found that certain materials help increase chip speed also.

Silicon is the most common of these materials (you've probably heard of silicon chips and Silicon Valley by now). Then there are the two elements germanium and selenium. And lately, the compound gallium arsenide (made from the elements gallium and arsenic) has shown promise in the search for better materials.

But besides materials, what else would help speed up a computer?

How about two computers running at once—couldn't they do twice the work in the same amount of time? Since entire CPU's can be fit onto individual chips, they can be connected and used simultaneously. You may have heard the term "math co-processor." That's an example of this parallel processing.

Also: Why not build just one CPU that *processes twice as much information at once?* A *word* is the group of bits a CPU processes at once. The bigger the word it can take at each pass, the faster it goes. Word sizes for PC processors are 16 bits or (more recently) 32 bits.

Making a More Useful Computer

Input

If you used large *mainframe* computers a few years ago, you went through a laborious process just to give it your instructions and data (input). You entered your program at a keypunch machine—punching holes on a *batch* of cards—exactly right and in perfect order. Then you presented your stack of cards to a clerk and waited hours—or even overnight—to get the printout. Then you took home the results of your efforts and puzzled until 3:00 a.m. trying to figure out what went wrong. The next day, you started over.

The first personal computer wasn't much easier. The Altair computer was introduced in 1975, but you wouldn't recognize it as a personal computer like those of today. It had no keyboard and no display—just a box with switches and lights on the front. You had to interpret program code and data yourself, then enter them into the computer by using the switches to enter individual bits. The panel lights gave your output in bits—which you then laboriously re-interpreted. Yuck!

The first computer that was actually easy to communicate with was the Apple, in 1976. It had a **keyboard** and could use a television as a **video display** —no more "bit-crunching" for the user!

Soon after came a slew of even better input devices: **Light pen**s, **touch-screens, joysticks** and **mice** are all efficient ways for you to input information into the computer. And automatic **sensors** can send physical data to the computer. **Digitizers** convert these signals into computer-usable bits. **Scanners** can read typewritten characters or copy pictures directly onto computer screens.

Output

Thankfully, long gone also is the time when you had to interpret panel lights to read the *results* of your computer's work. Now you have:

Monitors: The first IBM Personal Computer *monitor* (viewing screen) had only a foreground color and a background color—and no graphics, just characters. It was only *monochrome*, too; all of the characters were displayed in just one color. But now many color and graphics adapters are available, and the resolutions (the fine details) and the colors of their images vary considerably.

Printers: The first computer printers were *teletypewriters*—typewriters, originally made for telegraphs—that could transmit and receive signals to and from computers. These are the clackety things you hear in the background of old news shows. Then came *daisy-wheel* printers—like daisy-wheel typewriters—and just about as slow. Currently, the most-used kind of printer is the *dot-matrix* variety. Instead of a plastic daisy wheel of pre-formed characters, a matrix of tiny wires strike the inked ribbon to leave groups of dots on the paper. This method is much faster—and it can print graphics (lines and pictures) as well as characters. *Ink-jet* printers do the same thing, except that they literally spurt ink dots at the paper. *Laser printers* are currently the best printers available for personal computers. They form images with toner—much like a photocopying machine.

Plotters: A plotter is a special type of printer used, generally, for drafting. Instead of a typewriter-like ribbon, a mechanical pen is moved about on the paper and diagrams and characters are drawn at specified locations.

External Storage

As computers became popular, people soon learned how useful they were for storing information. Data bases grew, and now entire encyclopedias—even libraries—can be kept in computers.

An early storage method was **paper tape**. Like punched cards, strips of paper could also be punched with holes to represent a program or information. This method wasn't very durable or convenient.

Another solution was **magnetic tape**—the same method used to record music on cassettes. The bits are simply series of blips on the tapes. If the magnetism goes one way, the bit is *1*; if it's the other way, it's a *0*. One advantage of tapes is that they are non-volatile: The information is retained even when the computer is off. A disadvantage is that *random* access is impossible. You have to go through the whole tape to get to information at the other end of it (that's *serial* access).

Magnetic disks are currently the method of choice. The computer can go directly to any part of the disk to write or read information.

Disks are either *fixed* or *removable. Fixed* ("hard") disks are sealed in a dust-free environment where they can achieve better speed, accuracy and capacity. Fixed disks come in a wide range of sizes and capacities.

The *floppy disk* or diskette is a *removable* disk which is physically flexible. In older computers, the 8-inch size was popular, but now the 5.25-inch size is standard. And the *microdisk* (3.5-inch) is steadily replacing that as the most popular removable disk. It is more durable (it has a plastic casing), more convenient (it fits in a shirt pocket), and holds more information than 5.25-inch floppies.

Magnetic disks aren't the only kinds of disks in the computer arena now. The **CD ROM** is becoming ever more popular.

"CD" stands for *Compact **D**isk*.

Yes—it's the same CD technology that makes the beautiful "scratch-free" music in CD stereo systems. It's all just a bunch of bits: Whether it's music or a spreadsheet simply depends on how those bits are interpreted by the machine that reads them. CD uses laser technology to detect bumps on the disk. Changes in the bumps indicate the bits.

A CD ROM is a CD which has a Read Only Memory (just like a ROM chip). A CD ROM, is a removable disk, though, and can store the equivalent of several books. They are very durable, but are indeed "Read Only" (i.e. you can't put your own files on them. As yet, they're quite expensive, too.

The newest type of disk is the *erasable optical disk,* which shares the technology and storage capacity of the CD ROM, but which is *not* "Read Only." That is, its contents can be altered by the user—just like a standard fixed or floppy disk. And these incredible disks can store nearly six *hundred* books on one disk!

Computer History Mysteries*

1. Who invented bits?

2. What did Jacquard invent? How was it later adapted for use by computers?

3. Why does a computer lose its memory when it's turned off?

4. Are Boolean Algebra and the binary numbering system the same thing?

5. Suppose you were writing a program about cars. How could you represent the three car makes, "Ford," "Chevrolet," and "Dodge," using bits and bytes?

6. A computer can have a keyboard, a mouse, and other kinds of devices to use for input. It can also have a monitor, a printer, and other kinds of devices to use for output. How does the computer keep track of all these things in order to use them correctly?

*Yep—this is a quiz. Check your understanding now, before you go on to the next chapter. The answers are on the next page—but don't peek prematurely. Give these some thought.

History Mysteries Solved

1.   His name was Herman T. Bit.

        No—actually, bits were conceived in steps over a long period of
        time. Leibniz formally described the binary math system which
        used *1*'s and *0*'s. Then Boole created a logical system based on
        those two values. Shannon saw how both the math and the logic
        could apply to computers, and Atanasoff created the method for
        vacuum tubes to store them.

2.   Jacquard invented a loom which used punched cards to select the
        appropriately colored threads to make a design. Babbage then
        used punched cards for his mechanical calculator and Hollerith
        used them to assist in the 1890 U.S. Census.

3.   Whether a computer uses relays, vacuum tubes, transistors, or
        integrated circuits, a bit is represented by a current of electricity.
        When the current of electricity is gone, the status of the bit is lost.

4.   They are similar, but not exactly the same. They both use *1*'s and
        0's, but in a different way. The binary number system has to do
        with counting and math. Boolean Algebra has to do with logic.
        The key is, Boolean Algebra can be used to simulate binary math.
        This is what makes it possible for electrical circuits—which use
        Boolean Algebra—to "do math."

5. As a programmer, you can just assign certain combinations of the bits to represent the different types of cars:

```
01010101 = Ford
11110000 = Chevrolet
00001111 = Dodge
```

The exact combinations of the bits does not matter, just so that you consistently use the same bits to stand for the same type of car. Remember: You can make bits mean anything imaginable. How about these?

```
01010111 = Saturday's date
00110101 = A yacht
11111111 = Rad dude
```

6. A program (a set of *instructions*, or *software*) keeps track of all of these devices to use them correctly.

For example, you don't have to manually "tell" the computer how to draw characters on the monitor every time you want to see some output. There are special types of software, called *operating systems,* to handle these mundane tasks for you automatically.

Read the next chapter for more details....

2. CONTROLLING THE COMPUTER

Software

In the computer world, "soft" means "changeable," while "hard" means fixed or permanent. So *hard*ware is the actual, physical computer itself. Once you build the circuitry, keyboard, monitor, etc., that's it—you can't change it. But the instructions—all those bits stored in RAM that tell the CPU how to do things—those you *can* change. That's why programs (which are just lists of instructions) are called *soft*ware.

So you don't exactly have to "bronco-bust" a computer, but you do have to control it—with software, the real "smarts" of a computer. Fancy computer hardware is just expensive scrap metal without software.

Here are the main kinds of software:

- **Application Programs**—word processors, spreadsheets, databases, etc.—allow you to do specific kinds of work.

- **Operating Systems**, such as DOS, manage all of the background and organizational chores of your computer so you can concentrate on more important things—such as working with an application program.

- **Programming Languages** translate your instructions to the computer when you are *creating your own* application programs or operating systems.

This chapter introduces you to the last two kinds (you probably have a good "feel" already for what an applications program is).*

*If you'd rather get right to the "nuts and bolts" of learning DOS specifically, then you can go now to page 58—but you'll miss some good stuff!

The Turing Machine

Like many other aspects of computers, programs were conceived before there were any computers to try them.

In fact, an *imaginary* computer was created in order for scientists to write and study programs. This computer concept, called the Turing Machine, was introduced in 1936 by Englishman Alan Turing. Though it was never actually built—nor was it meant to be—it is justly famous.

The Turing Machine was an elegant mind game to help the scientists create the first computers (see the diagram on the next page):

- The Machine has an infinitely long paper tape running through it, containing *1*'s and *0*'s to represent bits.

- The Machine can *read* these bits *and change them* on the paper, according to certain rules—a kind of programming code. The diagram shows a list of those rules.

- A keyboard allows an operator to move the tape and change the bits also.

- The Machine has a dial to indicate which rule it is currently using, and a light on top to indicate when it is finished running.

The point is, the Turing Machine *schematically represents a general purpose computing device.* It can do anything the most modern computer can do!

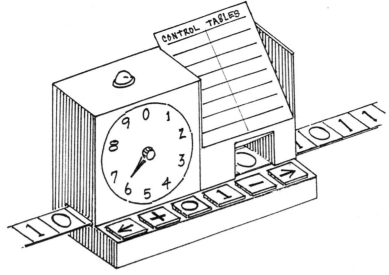

Look at a sample computing problem....

Problem: Compute the following Boolean **OR** operation:
0101 OR 0011

Solution: As you may remember from pages 22-23, the **OR** operation compares two bits at a time. When doing this by hand, it's easiest to place the two numbers vertically:

$$
\begin{array}{r}
0101 \\
\text{OR} \quad 0011 \\
\hline
\text{result:} \quad 0111
\end{array}
$$

See how this works? The **OR** operation compares the values *in each column* and assigns the appropriate result below that column. Do it like arithmetic—working column by column, starting on the right:

1 OR 1 = 1   **0 OR 1 = 1**   **1 OR 0 = 1**   **0 OR 0 = 0**

Now, how does the Turing Machine do that same problem?

First of all, it works in a straight row—left and right. So the problem is organized like this:

0101 0011 0001

The first value in the original problem (**0101**) is on the left here; the second value (**0011**) is in the middle.

The four bits on the right (**0001**) represent a "stop sign"—so that the Machine will know when it has finished working through the problem, bit by bit. When it has finished, the middle four bits will have been changed to reveal the answer.

As it works through the problem from left to right, the Machine uses these three rules to achieve an **OR** operation. Each rule depends upon whether the current bit is **0** or **1**:

	If Current Bit is **0**	If Current Bit is **1**
Rule 1	Go right 8 bits, use Rule 3.	Go right 4 bits, use Rule 2.
Rule 2	Change bit, go right 4 bits, use Rule 3.	Go right 4 bits, use Rule 3.
Rule 3	Go left 7 bits, use Rule 1.	Stop.

Now, *watch how this works.* The operation begins in Mode 1 at the left-most bit. Here goes:

	Situation	Current Bit	Rule	Action
Step 1:	0101 0011 0001	0	1	Right 8 bits, use Rule 3.
Step 2:	0101 0011 0001	0	3	Left 7 bits, use Rule 1.
Step 3:	0101 0011 0001	1	1	Right 4 bits, use Rule 2.
Step 4:	0101 0011 0001	0	2	Change bit, right 4 bits, use Rule 3.
Step 5:	0101 0111 0001	0	3	Left 7 bits, use Rule 1.
Step 6:	0101 0111 0001	0	1	Right 8 bits, use Rule 3.
Step 7:	0101 0111 0001	0	3	Left 7 bits, use Rule 1.
Step 8:	0101 0111 0001	1	1	Right 4 bits, use Rule 2.
Step 9:	0101 0111 0001	1	2	Right 4 bits, use Rule 3.
Step 10:	0101 0111 0001	1	3	Stop.

Voilá! The middle four bits are **0111**—the correct answer!

This Turing Machine example shows how a machine can be made to perform logical operations, using very simple rules, if it is *programmed* properly. It teaches the otherwise dumb machine how to behave in a *useful* way.

Programming (creating software) is the act of designing these instructions and the rules for their use. As you can see, this would be a *very* tedious process if you had to speak *0*'s and *1*'s all the time—and pay attention to every single move the machine has to make.

But you *don't* have to "speak binary" like this to instruct a machine....

Programs and Programming Languages

Fortunately, one of the first things computer people did to make life easier was to invent programming *languages*—programs that helped them *translate* their instructions into all those *1*'s and *0*'s.

Programming languages fall into various categories or *levels*—depending upon how much they can translate.

Machine Languages

For the computer itself, all instructions must be in raw bits and bytes—i.e. in *machine language*. This is a simple substitution code; certain combinations of bits stand for particular instructions.

For example, this sequence   **10110000 00000001**

tells a computer to put the value *1* into a certain location.

The computer reads this in sequence, one *byte* after another—just as a train comes into a station one car at a time. In the above example, the computer would first encounter the **10110000**, then the **00000001**. After having examined both bytes, it would take action, putting the value *1* into a certain location.

Well, as you can readily tell, machine language is virtually impossible for humans to work with, so they promptly invented a slightly higher-*level* language—and a program to translate between that language and these machine code ciphers.

Assembly Languages

To a computer, an *assembly language* is a foreign language—completely unintelligible. But it's more easily understood by human programmers than machine language, so they prefer it. And they use a program called an *assembler* to translate their assembler-level code into true machine language so that the computer will understand.

Here's a sample from an assembly language:

```
MOV    DL,20
MOV    CX,0060
MOV    AH,02
INT    21
INC    DL
LOOP   0107
INT    20
```

Well... it's a *little* bit more understandable to humans, though still quite cryptic. Each line tells the computer to take one action (though unless you know assembly language, you won't be able to figure out what those actions might be from just looking at these instructions).

The point is, learning this code is easier than staring at *1*'s and *0*'s all day. So assembly-level programmers type in these code words (which are stored in RAM simply as ASCII characters). Then they run the assembler, which translates those characters into machine language.

But if assembly language doesn't seem all that much easier than machine language, you're not alone. That's why there are even *higher*-level languages—which are even more like verbal instructions....

Interpreted and Compiled Languages

These types of programming languages use common English words to give programming instructions to a computer. They are much easier to use than assembly languages, but they can be slower.

Translation of these *high-level* ("easiest-to-use") languages down into machine language happens in two distinct ways:

- **Interpreting:** The high-level language is translated to machine language *as the program instructions are actually being executed* (i.e. as the program is *running*). This is like those simultaneous translations you hear when representatives speak at the United Nations. The version of the BASIC language that comes with DOS is a good example of an interpreted language.

- **Compiling:** The translation is all done before the program instructions are executed. This is like translating a book from a foreign language into your own. The conversion process is done only once—after which you always have the translation handy. Computer programmers call the original, untranslated program the *source code*, and the translated (machine language) version *object code*.

  As you might guess, compiled programs go much faster than interpreted programs because the translation has been done in advance. So most high-level programming languages, including Pascal, C, and FORTRAN are *compiled* languages.

Operating Systems

You can feel the power at your fingertips when you sit at a computer .... Integrated circuits, microprocessors, fast printers, graphics monitors, magnetic disks, compilers.

How do you *control* all this stuff ???

With an **operating system**.

An operating system is not just a program. It's a *collection* of specialized programs which help you control a computer. An operating system is many things to many people because it does so much. Operating systems can have five parts:

1. A *booting* program that starts the computer.

2. **B**asic **I**nput/**O**utput **S**ervices (BIOS) that handle and interpret the keyboard and other devices connected to the computer.

3. A *kernel* that allocates memory for other programs, loads them, and gets them going. Think of it as being a "colonel" in charge of getting things done.

4. A *shell* that communicates with the human operator. This is the part of *DOS* that receives your commands and acts on them.

5. Program *utilities* that provide additional services—such as an editor, a debugger, and other utilities.

What Operating Systems Do

An operating system helps you control your computer by making it more convenient to use:

- When you first turn on your computer, the operating system checks things to make sure everything is working properly, and then it loads itself into the computer's memory (RAM) to be able to serve you.

- When you start a program, the operating system finds a place for it in memory, puts it there, and then runs it.

- When you have many programs to keep track of, the operating system helps you do this.

- If a friend gives you a disk and you don't know what's on it, you can use operating system commands to find out.

- If you have an error in your computer system, the operating system will sometimes let you know.

- The operating system can give you password protection.

In short, your operating system saves you many headaches and much time by doing many of the "little things" that keep your work flowing smoothly.

Not only that, it can act similarly—as an assistant—*to other programs* (not just to human operators).

For example, a running application program can use commands called *system calls* (or *system interrupts*—so named because they interrupt the flow of the application program while communicating with the operating system). So when your word processor program executes a printing command (at your request), it may, in turn, sub-contract this job out—by calling upon the operating system to handle the printer. And while the operating system is doing that, the word-processing program is "interrupted;" it can't resume until the printing is done.

More noticeable, however, is when you communicate directly with your operating system, using one or more **commands** that you type. These commands fall into these general categories:

- Commands that manage disks.
- Commands that manage files.
- Commands that manage directories.
- Commands that manage devices.
- Commands that customize your computer.

Without knowing these commands, you'll get little benefit from your operating system; they are the keys to controlling your computer.

It may be hard to appreciate yet just how much an operating system will do for you, but don't take such control for granted!

It wasn't always so easy....

The Evolution of Operating Systems

In a sense, *you* are an operating system, too: You direct your computer's operations. But if you were the only operating system, you'd have *far too much to do*. With so many devices and parts of the computer to control (disk drives, monitors, and printers), how could you remember and direct every little thing the computer had to do—and then get any meaningful work done besides?

The early **batch** file (punched card) system was typical of this problem (remember that painful description on page 33?). You had to plan every little step ahead of time, punch the instructions onto cards—in the right order—then send this *batch* of cards to the computer. Because you were in charge of most of the housekeeping details—as well as the work you were trying to do—there were many opportunities for nit-picky mistakes. If you made a boo-boo, however minuscule, you'd have to repeat the procedure.

But as time went by, people developed ways to "smarten" computers with housekeeping programs to relieve you of all the details.

Buffers are one example: When a computer reads a disk, it reads a whole chunk of information at once and places it into an area of (RAM) memory called a *buffer*. The next time the same information is needed, it's right there in that RAM buffer—which is much "closer at hand"— thus speeding up the processing.

And as other devices—printers, monitors, keyboards—made input and output chores simpler for you, the computer had to know all the housekeeping details of those devices, too. So operating systems evolved to serve this need.

In fact, operating systems have become downright sophisticated now.

With hundreds, even thousands, of personal computers wired in networks—often involving large mainframe computers, too—operating systems have evolved into "traffic cops," making sure that authorized users get access to the mainframe and to other shared devices.

For such a "traffic-cop" network operating system, three different approaches are common:

- *Real-time operation.* A human operator can use the mainframe all by him/herself. He/she has the computer's complete attention *right now.* (Few people in a network get this privilege.)

- *Time-sharing operation.* The operating system allows many people to work with one mainframe. Their commands are placed into buffers, which the computer then handles one after the other, in rotation—often so fast that it *appears* to be real-time to any given person.

- *Multiprocessing.* This is the most common arrangement today for personal computers. People use their personal computers for the normal stuff, and call on the mainframe only for the tough jobs. The operating system handles those calls in a manner similar to time-sharing.

The explosion of personal computers on the market in the late 1970's created a new problem in the evolution of operating systems:

How could application programmers write software that would work on all of these different types of machines? Previously, *standardized* operating systems hadn't been all that necessary. But when the computer began to get into the hands of ordinary consumers—instead of computer professionals—things had to change.

The solution? **CP/M** (Control **P**rogram for **M**icrocomputers). This was the first really standardized operating system; it could be run on different brands of computers, so that one application program, written for CP/M, could run on a variety of low-priced machines.

For awhile, CP/M was the standard operating system for personal computers. Then in 1981, IBM introduced its *Personal Computer* which ran on the *DOS* operating system. With IBM's overwhelming impact on the marketplace, CP/M soon went the way of the slide rule.* And the rest, as they say, is history.

---

*The slide rule was something like a wooden calculator, with three rulers placed side-by-side and the middle ruler sliding between the other two. These rulers were marked off in logarithmic intervals, and so it was theoretically possible to do math by sliding the middle ruler left and right and comparing the "logs." But actually, students just put them in long leather cases which dangled from their belts. Then one day, electronic calculators appeared, multiplied like rabbits, and slide rules vanished from the planet.

Check Your Softawareness

1. Which part of software is actually "soft?"

2. What's the difference between "software" and "program"?

3. How many Turing Machines are currently in existence?

4. Do programming languages eliminate the need for machine language?

5. What's the difference between interpreters and compilers?

6. How are operating systems and programs similar?

7. Suppose you have many reports that you have written on a word processor. You want to organize them on your disk as you would papers in a file cabinet. How would you do this?

Softawarenecessities

1.   Software is all "soft." That is, since it is a collection of instruc-
      tions created by human beings, it is all readily *changeable*—unlike
      the nuts and bolts of your machine's hardware.

2.   "Software" and "program" mean the same thing.

3.   No Turing Machine was ever actually made. It was a mind game
      to help scientists conceive and design computers. The Turing
      Machine is very durable (no moving parts!): It's still used in
      computer theory.

4.   Programming languages do not eliminate machine language.
      They simply let you avoid *dealing with* machine language. All
      programs and software must be in machine language before they
      can be run by a computer, so programming languages *translate*
      your commands into machine language so that they can be run
      by the computer.

5.   Both interpreters and compilers are types of programming
      languages. Interpreters translate program code to machine
      language each time a program is run. Compilers just do it once;
      thereafter, the program remains in machine language.

6. An operating system is just a specialized program which assists you in controlling a computer. It does five things:

   (i) It gets the computer going when turned on.

   (ii) It handles the technical chores of controlling the keyboard and other input/output devices.

   (iii) It allocates memory for other programs, loads them, and gets them started.

   (iv) It communicates with the human operator through commands and messages.

   (v) It often provides utility services, such as text editors, program debuggers, etc.

7. You would use your operating system's commands and tell it to create directories for the various types of reports you've written. Then you would create a file for each of the reports and put the proper files into the proper directories.

   Exactly how you would do this kind of thing (and many other worthy projects) with *one specific kind* of operating system—**DOS**—is the subject of the remainder of this Course.

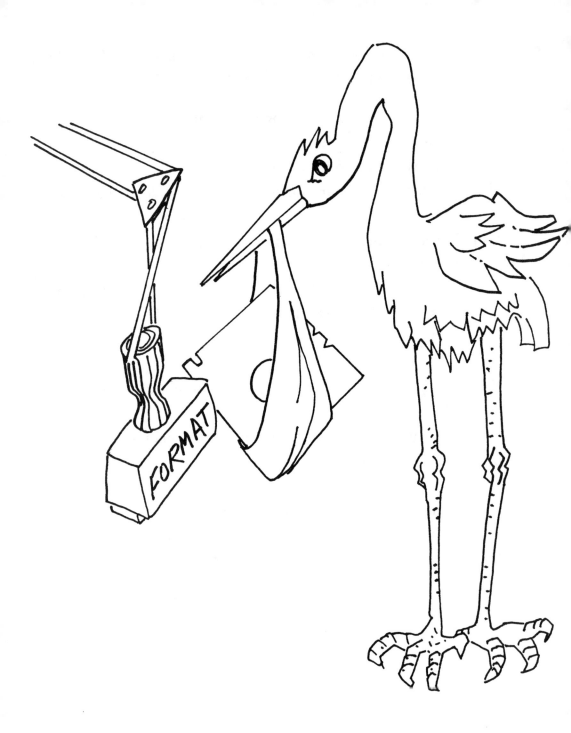

3. KEY CONCEPTS IN DOS

Your Computer System

The "stork" has brought you a brand-spanking-new computer. Now what? First, learn a little more about it....

Your CPU

Imagine an old rolltop desk: You take things out of the cubbyholes, or an "in" basket, and place them in the center, where you work on them. When you're done, you might put them back (or in an "out" basket).

The **C**entral **P**rocessing **U**nit (CPU), located on the main "chip" in your machine, occupies the center of your "desk"—where the work really gets done. Just as you shuffle papers around on the desktop as you're working on them, so the CPU shuffles bytes around between its various *registers* as it works on the task at hand.

How fast it can do this shuffling depends on two main things—its *word size* and its *clock speed*. Word size (see page 32) is the number of bits your CPU can handle at one time; the more it can handle at once, the faster the work gets done. When computer pros describe CPU's as "8-bit, 16-bit, or 32-bit processors," they're referring to the word sizes.

Clock speed refers to the rate at which the CPU handles its words—one word per cycle. Some common speeds are 8MHz, 12MHz, 16 MHz, and 25 MHz. The "MHz" means *megahertz*, or million cycles per second. Some computer instructions can be done in one cycle, but most require several cycles. Three popular CPU's are the 80286, 80386 and 80486. The larger the number, the better the CPU.

Your Main Memory

The "cubbyholes" in your computer "desk" comprise your main memory —your RAM (see page 30). As it works, your CPU transfers large chunks of bytes—programs, instructions, data, and ASCII text—to and from these "RAM cubbyholes."

The size of this memory is measured in kilobytes (Kb or just K). The more, the better, usually—and most computers allow you to add extra RAM (i.e. more RAM chips) if you need it.

Your Peripherals

The peripherals to your computer, also called *devices*, act as your "in" and "out" baskets.

- "In" baskets include all *input* devices—keyboards, mice, scanners and any other *devices that send work to the CPU.*

- "Out" baskets include all *output* devices—monitors, printers, and any other *devices that receive the finished work from the CPU.*

Your Monitor

Of these peripheral devices, the one you interact with the most is the monitor. You should know exactly what kind of monitor you have, because it can affect how you interact with *DOS* and with other programs you use.

Monitors are best described in terms of *pixels*, which are single dots on the video display that comprise all characters and images. The more pixels you can squeeze onto the screen, the better the resolution of these characters and images. Here's a table of the common types of monitors and their typical pixel counts. The table progresses from poor quality at the top to excellent quality at the bottom.

Type of monitor		Across x Down	=	Total Pixels
CGA –	Color Graphics Adapter	640 x 200	=	128,000
EGA –	Enhanced Graphics Adapter	640 x 350	=	224,000
Mono –	Monochrome	720 x 350	=	252,000
Herc –	Hercules Graphics Adapter	720 x 350	=	252,000
VGA –	Video Graphics Array	640 x 480	=	307,200

While this table gives you an idea about how good the different types of monitors are, it does not show all of the possibilities. How many pixels a monitor displays can also depend on how many colors are being displayed at once and whether or not graphics are being used.

Besides pixels, other things to be considered are color and graphics:

- Color. The Mono and Herc monitors display just one color. The CGA can display 4 colors at once; the EGA, 16; and the VGA, 256.

- Graphics. The Mono cannot do graphics. The others can.

Now, what's another kind of computer peripheral that functions both as an "in" basket and "out" basket?...   How about...

Your Disk Drives

You may have one or more disk drives connected to your machine. It pays to know exactly what kind they are.

- They might be *floppy drives*—meaning they accept removable 5.25-inch floppy disks.

- They might be *microdisk drives*—meaning they accept the newer, smaller, 3.5-inch removable microdisks.

- They might be *external fixed drives*—meaning that they are sitting next to your computer attached to it by a cable and, unlike drives for removable disks, have no openings for disks at all.

- They might be *internal fixed drives*—meaning that they are sealed inside your computer.

- They might be *high capacity laser drives*—like the CD ROM disk drives and erasable optical disk drives that use removable disks resembling a standard musical compact disk.

Each kind of removable-disk drive (the first two listed above) comes in another kind of variation as well: a *standard* (or *low-density*)* drive or a *high-density* (HD) drive. The difference between these is simply the amount of data you can squeeze onto each side of the disk.

---

*Actually, these drives, and the disks designed to be used in them, are often referred to as *double-density*. This can be confusing when you're shopping for blank disks. Double-density (DD) is actually the *lower* density category.

And then naturally, it takes a different type of disk *drive* to use each of these various kinds of disks:

- The standard floppy drive cannot write in "high density."

- The high-density floppy drive was made for 1.2-Mb* high-density floppy disks.**

- The standard microdisk drive uses standard 720K microdisks.

- The high-density microdisk can be used safely with either the standard (720K) or the high-density (1440K) disk drive. Of course, if you spent the extra money for a high-density drive, you'll probably want to use high-density disks, so that you won't have so many disks to keep track of.

Good Grief

No matter what kinds of devices your computer has, they all have one thing in common: The work they send or receive is in *bytes*. And with all of these bytes zipping around inside the computer, a manager is needed to determine what goes where and when. This manager is a crucial piece of your computer system. This manager is (guess who?)...

---

*Mb stands for "megabyte." It is sometimes abbreviated to M or Meg. Technically, a Mb is 1,048,576 bytes, but many people round it to 1,000 K. Thus, although not correct arithmetically, 1,200 K and 1.2 Mb usually mean the same thing.

**A 1.2-Mb high-density floppy drive can *use* standard floppy disks, but those disks are not always readable by a standard drive afterwards. There are some high-density drives available that have corrected this problem.

Your Operating System—DOS

"DOS" is just a nickname for "**D**isk **O**perating **S**ystem."

DOS has two formal ("brand") names:*

- PC-DOS (for "**P**ersonal **C**omputer" **DOS**)
- MS-DOS (for "**M**icrosoft" **DOS**)

Here's why: When IBM began selling personal computers, it sold DOS with the computers. IBM gave DOS a special name. It was called PC-DOS—named after the "PC" (the IBM Personal Computer)—although the software was still owned by Microsoft Corporation, and IBM paid Microsoft a fee for distributing DOS.

Then, when the IBM-compatibles hit the market, they also needed DOS. Microsoft couldn't sell them PC-DOS, because that referred to IBM's computer specifically. So Microsoft sold everybody else MS-DOS—virtually the same thing but with a different name!

Now, though, many people have given up referring to it as PC-DOS and/or MS-DOS—they just call it by the generic name, DOS.

So a "DOS computer" is any computer which runs some version of DOS. This includes the IBM Personal Computer and its upgrades and compatibles.

---

*Digital Research, who made CP/M (recall page 54), is trying to get back into the action with DR-DOS, which is a copycat of MS-DOS. (But then, MS-DOS copied many features of CP/M, so it's hard to say who's copying whom.)

The proper name of DOS includes the version number—sort of a model number.

The computer software model numbering system is sometimes called the "Dewey Decimal System of software," because it's used by virtually all types of software—not just DOS.

The numbering system has the form **X.YZ**.

- An increase in the **"X"** digit means that a revision's changes were very extensive; the newer version is virtually a total "rewrite" of the previous version. For example, DOS 4.00 was virtually rewritten from DOS 3.00; the changes were very substantial.

- An increase in the **"Y"** digit means that minor but significant changes were made. For example, DOS 3.2 added some features which DOS 3.1 did not have—but it was not a complete rewrite of the previous version.

- A change in the **"Z"** digit means that very minor changes were made. DOS 4.01 and DOS 4.00 are virtually the same thing.

The five major versions of DOS particularly stand out (the unidentified digits YZ mean that each of these major versions has been modified in minor or very minor ways occasionally during its "life"):

Version 1.YZ: This relic of the past was introduced with the original IBM Personal Computer. Virtually nobody uses this version anymore, because it can't handle fixed disks nor the popular 360-kilobyte 5.25-inch floppy disks. You should not be concerned with Version 1.YZ at all.

Version 2.YZ: This was one of the most widely distributed versions of DOS because it does support fixed disks and 360-kilobyte 5.25-inch floppy disks. Almost all applications programs require Version 2.YZ or higher.

Version 3.YZ: This added support for the smaller 3.5-inch disks, and high-density disks and networks.

Version 4.YZ: This added a menu display that is compatible with a mouse. It also allows for more convenient use of extremely large fixed disks.

Version 5.YZ: This added a help system, a new editor, additional memory support, and numerous other features.

If all this DOS detail worries you, consider this: You can be pretty knowledgeable about cars and not know anything about, say, a '59 Caddy. And it's the same with DOS: There's simply no reason to worry about all the differences between all of the versions. If you need to know something about one or more particular versions, this book will point it out at the time.

Do This: Now that you know a little more about your computer system, its peripheral devices, see if you can fill in the list below. If you need to peek at your owner's manuals, that's OK; you'll find this list handy later in this Course.

Central Processing Unit (CPU)

Name: _____

Word Size: _____

Clock Speed: _____

Memory

RAM Available: _____

Peripherals

Input devices connected

1. _____

2. _____

3. _____

Video Monitor and Adapter: _____

Disk drives connected

1. _____

2. _____

3. _____

4. _____

Output devices connected

1. _____

2. _____

3. _____

DOS Version: _____

Introduction to Files

As your computer system's "manager," DOS handles many of the bytes zipping around in the computer by grouping them together into files. A file is simply a sequence of bytes ...

> ... like the beads in a necklace...
> ... like the sections in a fence ...
> ... like the squares in a sidewalk.

Files can be moved to many places inside a computer. You can create a file at the keyboard and send it to the monitor, to the printer, or to a disk. And DOS gives you the commands you need to move and manipulate files like this, but before you can learn all that, you need to know how to specify which files you want....

A *filename* consists of two parts—and you must specify both parts of the filename to access a file:

- The first part is the *name* itself, which may be up to eight characters long.

- Then comes the *extension,* a three-character abbreviation that often helps classify the file into a category. These two parts are separated by a period (.).

For example, the file **MSDOS.SYS** has a name (**MSDOS**) and an extension or category (**SYS**).

A filename's extension can indicate what kind of file *structure* the file has—that is, how its bytes should be interpreted. For example, a common structure for word processing files is the **ASCII** code. As you may recall from page 25, **ASCII** is one common way to convert between characters meaningful to humans and bytes meaningful to computers.

But **ASCII** isn't the only structure used. For example, the *WordPerfect* program doesn't use a pure **ASCII** structure in its files. It adds special bytes to represent boldface, underlines, and other ways of changing text. The *WordPerfect* programmers decided exactly which bytes would be used for which purposes. And programmers of other word processors chose other sets of bytes to do those same things. That's why files created on one word processor are often unusable on another.

Problem: If you write a document on one brand of word processor, how do you then use it with another???

Solution #1:   Some special programs have been written to *translate* from one type of file structure to another .

Solution #2:   Almost all word processors let you save and read files in pure **ASCII** code—besides the structure unique to that program. So you could save your document in **ASCII** code from one word processor, then retrieve it as **ASCII** code into the other word processor.

So **ASCII** is a generic, common-denominator standard often used as a go-between among various file structures. In fact, in this Course, you'll be using DOS to create some **ASCII** text files.

Essential DOS Files

DOS is made up of files—lots of 'em. Getting to know the DOS files helps you to get to know DOS....

On page 49, you read that operating systems have five characteristics. Now look at how DOS fulfills the requirements of each of those characteristics—with files:

1. "A booting program that starts the computer."

   This program is the very first series of instructions the computer finds when it powers up. These instructions live in a file at the beginning of a *disk*—not inside the machine itself. This file doesn't have a formal name, but is sometimes called the *boot record* or *boot sector*.

2. "Basic Input/Output Services (BIOS) that handle and interpret the keyboard and other devices connected to the computer."

   This is the **IO.SYS** file, again, located on the disks used to start up the computer. The **IO.SYS** file is loaded into memory (RAM) where it remains to do its work.

   On IBM-brand computers, this file is named **IBMBIO.COM**.

3. "A kernel that allocates memory for other programs, loads them, and gets them going. Think of it as being a 'colonel' in charge of getting things done."

This is the **MSDOS.SYS** file—also found on those disks you use to start up the computer. It, too, is loaded into memory (RAM) where it stays to do its work.

On IBM-brand computers, this file is named **IBMDOS.COM**.

4. "A shell that communicates with the human operator. This is the part of DOS that receives your commands and acts on them."

This is the **COMMAND.COM** file, which exists on the startup disks.* It is often placed in memory (RAM), but is sometimes overwritten by other programs, in which case you get a message on the video screen.

5. "Program utilities that provide additional services—such as an editor, a debugger, and other utilities."

In *DOS Version 5.0*, this includes 55 different files—but don't panic. You'll learn about the important ones all in good time in this Easy Course.

---

*DOS Versions 4.00 and greater also contain a second shell named "The DOS Shell," which is scattered about in various files containing the word "shell" in their names.

In addition, there are two other important DOS files—but *you* have to make them up yourself—which you'll soon learn how to do:

- **CONFIG.SYS**

  This stands for **CONFIG**ure **SYS**tem. The **CONFIG.SYS** file contains a list of certain settings which you can use to customize (i.e. configure) your computer, according to your own preferences—and the hardware and peripherals you happen to have.

- **AUTOEXEC.BAT**

  This stands for **AUTO**matically **EXEC**utable **BAT**ch file. You set up this file so that certain mundane tasks are done *automatically* every time you start your computer.

Disks and Formats

Just as files have structures for giving meaning to their bytes, so disks have *formats*, in which they store files. Knowing something about these formats helps you to be an expert in controlling your computer.

A *disk format* is a method of dividing a disk storage space into manageable units—like filing cabinets, drawers, and manila folders. A disk format has three components:

Tracks: A single track on a disk is a circle around the disk—like a lane on a circular freeway. Floppy disks typically have 40 tracks per side; microdisks, 80.

Sectors: Each track is divided into sectors—like arc segments of a circle. There are 9 sectors per track for removable disks. A single sector usually contains 512 bytes.

Clusters: A cluster is the amount of information read or written to a disk at a time. Common cluster sizes are 2 or 4 sectors.

Here are summaries of two formats—those of the 5.25" floppy and the 3.5" microdisk—that are particularly popular:

Disk	bytes per sector	x	sectors per track	x	tracks per side	x	Sides	= Bytes	
Floppy	512	x	9	x	40	x	2	= 368,640	= 360K
Micro	512	x	9	x	80	x	2	= 737,280	= 720K

Before it can be used by the computer, each disk must be formatted. That is, blank sectors in each track must be laid out—like freshly plowing a field before planting.

As you might suspect, this formatting will destroy all the previous information on a disk. So you should format a disk only to prepare *new* disks or to completely *erase* and recycle old disks.

Here's what happens when a disk is formatted:

1. A *boot record* is created in the first cluster.

2. A **F**ile **A**llocation **T**able (**FAT**) is created. The FAT contains technical information about where files are located on the disk, cluster by cluster (a single file may be scattered in clusters all over a disk). The FAT also keeps a record of any damaged clusters on a disk.

3. A *disk directory* is created to record the length and date of each file on the disk.

4. The remainder of the disk is *erased*.

5. Each sector is *tested*; bad ones are recorded in the FAT so that they won't be used.

Introduction to Commands

Formatting helps prepare disks for file storage. But that's only the beginning: You have all of those peripheral devices to worry about, all those files to move and change—and different kinds of disks! How do you handle it all?

The answer is: **DOS commands**. You command DOS to take care of these things for you!

Of course, DOS won't do *everything* (it won't cook you a hamburger), so you have to know which commands DOS will obey. And how does DOS "know" a command? It looks for a *file* by that name and executes the instructions in that file. So part of knowing how to give commands to DOS is knowing *where* DOS will find those command files to run when you request them. There are two possible places:

- In the computer's memory (RAM), in the file called `COMMAND.COM` (see page 71) there are up to 28 DOS commands—all merged together within one large file. And since this large `COMMAND.COM` stays in RAM, these 28 commands are available all the time and are called *internal* commands.

- On disks, each in its own individual file named for that command, live many more DOS commands. All told, in DOS versions 1.0 through 5.0, there are some 55 of these commands (not all versions have all 55). Since they are outside of RAM, these are *external* commands—and *the disk containing an external command must be in the disk drive in order to use that command.*

So, how do you know which commands are internal and which are external? You look at these lists:

The 28 internal commands:

BREAK	CTTY	LH	RMDIR	TYPE
CHCP	DATE	LOADHIGH	RD	VERIFY
CHDIR	DEL	MKDIR	REN	VER
CD	DIR	MD	RENAME	VOL
CLS	ERASE	PATH	SET	
COPY	EXIT	PROMPT	TIME	

The 55 external commands:*

APPEND	DISKCOMP	FIND	LOADFIX	SELECT
ASSIGN	DISKCOPY	FDISK	MEM	SETUP
ATTRIB	DOSKEY	FORMAT	MIRROR	SETVER
BACKUP	DOSSHELL	GRAPHICS	MODE	SHARE
BASIC	EDIT	GRAFTABL	MORE	SORT
BASICA	EDLIN	GWBASIC	NLSFUNC	SUBST
CHKDSK	EMM386	HELP	PRINT	SYS
COMMAND	EXE2BIN	JOIN	QBASIC	TREE
COMP	EXPAND	KEYB	RECOVER	UNDELETE
DEBUG	FASTOPEN	LABEL	REPLACE	UNFORMAT
DELOLDOS	FC	LINK	RESTORE	XCOPY

Right now, this probably looks like alphabet soup, no? Don't fret—this Course will introduce you to them all in due time.

*External commands are often called *utilities*. Don't let this throw you—they mean the same thing.

How to Use Commands

In fact, *before you even turn on your machine,* you can learn a lot about commands—just by reading here....

VER: This command asks what **VER**sion of DOS your computer is using. You simply type the command's name, (**VER**)* and the computer will display the name of its DOS version.

Easy, right? Indeed, most DOS commands have more to them than this. They're not single words but whole "sentences." And like English sentences, they have a grammar of sorts—a ***command syntax.***

When you learned English, you saw how to put nouns, verbs, adverbs, and adjectives together in order to communicate with people. Similarly, with DOS command syntax, you must put key words, parameters, switches, and operators together to communicate with DOS. And it's not all that difficult—there's some rhyme and reason to it.

FORMAT: This command formats a new disk or reformats an old one. But you can't just type **FORMAT** and expect the computer to do something. It needs to know more than just the name of the command; it needs to know what *particular* disk you want to format.

---

*You may type commands in either uppercase or lowercase. This Easy Course will use uppercase.

But even before that, your computer will want to know where to *find* the **FORMAT** command.

Hmm...: Why doesn't the computer need to know where to find the **VER** command—but it does need to know where to find **FORMAT**?

Aha: Look at the list of commands on page 76. **VER** is an *internal* command; the computer always has it stored in memory where it can find it. **FORMAT**, on the other hand, is an *external* command, so the computer needs to be directed to the disk containing the **FORMAT** file.

So, how do you tell the computer where to find the **FORMAT** command file? First, *you* need to know where it is. If it's on a removable disk (floppy or micro), then put that disk into a disk drive. If it's on your fixed disk, you needn't do anything—the "disk" is already loaded.

Then, you need to tell the computer the *path* to the **FORMAT** file.

The first part of the path to the **FORMAT** file is the name of the disk drive that has the correct disk in it. The *drive identifier* is a single letter followed by a colon (**:**). Typically, the **A:** drive is a removable disk drive (for floppies or microdisks); the **B:** drive will mean a second removable disk drive; and the **C:** drive will mean a fixod disk drive.

So when you specify a disk drive *before* a command, it indicates to *DOS* where to look for that command.

OK: If you put the disk containing the **FORMAT** file into the **A:** disk drive and type in **A:FORMAT**, this would do it, then—no?

No: Getting to the right disk is only the first step. Next you need to get to the right *directory*. **Directories** are like manila folders—that organize and separate specific collections of files. And yes—directories can be buried in other directories, just as folders can be buried in other folders.

You denote a directory in DOS with a backslash (****). Each disk has a main directory, called the **root directory**. To get to this root directory, you just add the backslash to the name of the drive it's in. For example, to specify the root directory of the disk in the **A:** drive, you'd type **A:**.

But: How would you send the computer to a sub-directory (i.e. a "folder within a folder") called **DOS** that's located in the root directory of the disk in the **A:** drive?

OK: You would type **A:\DOS**

So the **pathname** of a file is essentially a list of the storage places the computer needs to go through (i.e. the "path" it needs to follow) to find the file:

disk drive **:** **** *subdirectory* **** *file*

with each new "folder" level denoted by a backslash (****).

Thus, if the **FORMAT** file is located in the root directory of the disk in the **A:** drive, you would direct the computer to it by typing its entire *pathname:* **A:\FORMAT**

Or, if the **FORMAT** file is located in a subdirectory—called DOS—of the root directory of your fixed disk (in the **C:** drive), you would direct the computer to it by typing *that* pathname: **C:\DOS\FORMAT**

Get the idea? This is how, for *external* commands, you use the *entire pathname* of the command, thereby directing the computer to the location of that command file . And of course, for *internal* commands (such as **VER**), you need only use the abbreviated name of the command (its *keyword*), since the computer already knows where to find that command—in the **COMMAND.COM** file in RAM.*

So, if you use the pathname of the **FORMAT** command, is that enough? Not until you tell it in *which* drive to find the disk to be formatted.

Most commands (**VER** is one of the few exceptions) need more information than simply where the command file is located. And each such piece of information is called a ***parameter***.

The **FORMAT** command needs one parameter—the name of the disk drive where the disk to be formatted is located.

---

*Some computers have DOS on a ROM chip instead of on disks. With these computers, all the DOS commands appear to be internal, and you do not have to give DOS the pathnames to external commands.

DOS uses a space to separate each parameter—so don't ignore the spaces in these commands! To complete the command "sentence" for the **FORMAT** command, you need to add a space and a parameter:

A:\FORMAT A:

Now, this would work: The computer would find the **FORMAT** file on the disk in the root directory of the **A** drive and follow the instructions in that file, formatting the blank disk you'll then place into the **A:** drive.

Question: What happens if you don't include the required parameters for a command?

Answer: It depends on what kind of parameter it is. If you left out the name of a disk drive (say, in the **FORMAT** command), then the computer may *automatically substitute* the name of the *current* drive—the last drive you directed it to. These computer substitutions are known collectively as ***defaults***. Usually, the computer uses the current directory as the default path parameter, and the current disk drive as the default disk drive parameter.

Sometimes the computer checks with you first before using a default.* Sometimes it doesn't. Sometimes it will give you an error message, meaning you should try the command again more carefully.

---

*For example, if your current drive is the fixed drive (**C:**) and you forget to specify which drive to use for formatting, the computer may ask you to confirm that you really do want to erase your 80 Megabytes of data stored on the *current* disk. If you're lucky, you may get a chance to "just say **no**!"

So in order for commands to work, you must include *keywords* (with or without their *pathnames*) and all required *parameters* (such as substitutions for the default parameters). These are the "nouns" and "verbs" of command "sentences."

But many commands come with options that you can select to cause the command to behave differently from one time to the next. One category of options are the built-in, pre-designed **switches** that you can add to the command "sentence."

FORMAT has one common switch (the **/S** switch):

A:\FORMAT A: /S

When you use this switch with the **FORMAT** command like this, the DOS system files are automatically placed onto the new blank disk after it has been formatted. This makes the new disk a *system disk* and allows you to use it to start the computer.

Notice that switches use slashes (**/**) while pathnames use backslashes (****). Confusing these two marks is probably the most common error you'll make using DOS.

You've learned a lot this chapter. How much really stuck with you?...

Don't Lose Your Keys!

1. If you were to draw an analogy between your computer and a desk, which part would be the CPU? What would be the "in" and "out" baskets?

2. What's the difference between MS-DOS, PC-DOS, and DOS?

3. What's the difference between internal and external commands?

4. Why does a disk need to be formatted?

5. What's the difference between a filename and a pathname?

6. *Challenge:* You have just one disk drive, the **A:** drive (so it's automatically the default drive). What's the shortest **FORMAT** command you can use?

7. *Super Challenge:* Using a fixed disk, can you think of a way to make external commands appear to be internal, thus making them more convenient to use?

Checking for Your Keys

1. The CPU would be the center of the desk where the actual work gets done. The "in" baskets would be the input devices—the keyboard and mouse. The "out" baskets would be the output devices—monitor, printer, etc. A disk drive is both an "in" and an "out" basket.

2. They all refer to the same thing. MS-DOS is the official name of the operating system, given to it by Microsoft Corporation, who developed it. PC-DOS refers to that same operating system when it is sold with IBM-brand computers. DOS is the generic term used to refer to either one—or both.

3. *Internal* commands are a part of the **COMMAND.COM** program file which is loaded into memory when the computer is turned on. Since they stay in the computer's memory, internal commands are "built-in" and ready for use at any time. *External* commands are separate programs. Like application programs, such as word processors, the disk containing the external command must in the disk drive before the computer can run it.

4. A brand new disk is not ready to be used by the computer because it doesn't have a boot record, File Allocation Table (FAT), and root directory. Also, DOS needs to check all of the areas on the new disk to make sure they're good enough to be used.

5. Both types of names identify files.

A *filename* consists of two parts, the name (a maximum of eight characters) and the extension (three characters), which are separated by a period (.). **COMMAND.COM** is a filename you've seen in this chapter.

A *pathname* includes the path by which the computer finds a file—a more complete identification than the filename. For example, **C:\TEXT\LETTER\TOGEORGE.TXT** is a pathname that could lead the computer to the file containing your letter to Uncle George (**TOGEORGE.TXT**).

6. The shortest command would be, simply, **FORMAT**. DOS would look for the external **FORMAT** command in the **A:** drive (the default) and would format a disk in the same drive* (still the default). Note that since the **/S** switch was omitted, the newly formatted disk could *not* be used to start the computer, since the newly-formatted disk would not contain any of the essential DOS system startup files.

7. Picture this: Put the external commands on the fixed disk, and make that fixed disk the *default* disk drive. You can even put the *DOS* commands in their own special directory on the fixed disk and make this directory accessible no matter what the defaults are. This Easy Course will soon teach how to do all of this.

---

*Of course, DOS would display a message telling you to switch disks before starting the formatting process, so that you don't format the wrong disk.

4. GETTING UP TO SPEED

Installing DOS: The First Time

You have to get your computer going in order to learn about DOS—but you have to know about DOS to get your computer going.*

What a dilemma! To get past this Catch-22, take a break from learning what the commands mean—just follow directions for a while. It'll be clear when you need to start understanding-as-you-go once again. But until then, just follow the recipe....

What You Need:

- DOS (if DOS didn't come with your computer, you may have to go to a computer or software store and purchase it).

- From 2 to 15 new, blank disks (depending on the version of DOS and the capacities of the disks you have).

- Disk labels (address labels work fine).

- A felt tip pen to write on the labels (ballpoint pens can ruin disks).

*If you're already running DOS on your computer, it means that it's already installed. Review how this course installs it for your type of disk (fixed or removable) and then skip to page 95.

Which Case Are You?

How you install DOS depends on which version you have and whether you have a fixed disk. Each case below covers one possibility. Just decide which case applies to you and follow those instructions.*

Case 0: Your computer has DOS *pre-installed* on a ROM chip. If this is your case, all of the commands will appear to be internal and any instructions referring to DOS disks will not apply to you. Skip all of the installation instructions and go directly to page 95.

Case 1: DOS is on a set of disks, one of them labelled *Install*. You have no fixed disk (only removable disks). Go to the next page.

Case 2: DOS is on a set of disks, one of them labelled *Install*. You do have a fixed disk. Go to page 90.

Case 3: DOS is on a set of disks, *none* of them labelled *Install*. You have no fixed disk (only removable disks). Go to page 91.

Case 4: DOS is on a set of disks, *none* of them labelled *Install*. You do have a fixed disk. Go to page 92.

---

*When installing DOS, you may or may not be asked to enter volume labels. If you are, enter **DOS**.

Installation Instructions

Case 1: DOS is on a set of disks, one of them labelled *Install*. You have no fixed disk (only removable disks).

Step 1: Put the *Install* disk into the A: disk drive and start the computer.

Step 2: Follow the directions on the video screen. It may ask you to switch disks, enter information about your system (your printer, keyboard, etc.), and allow you to choose between certain options. If you're asked, the following options are recommended:

- **Maximum DOS function**
- **Accept predefined keyboard**
- **Install DOS on Drive A***
- **Install the DOS Shell**
- **Accept Configuration**

This installation process will take several minutes. Then, go to page 94.

---

* Note: If you install DOS on the B: drive and the disks in the B: drive don't fit in the A: drive (because they're differently sized disks), then the startup disk won't properly start your computer.

Case 2:   DOS is on a set of disks, one of them labelled *Install*. You do have a fixed disk.

Step 1:   Find out if your fixed disk has been **partitioned**. Partitions logically divide fixed disks into major units. A brand-new fixed disk must be partitioned before it can be used— unless the dealer has done it for you. *If there are files on your fixed disk, it's already partitioned. Partitioning it again will erase those files.* If your fixed disk is not already partitioned when you use the *Install* disk, the video screen will ask you how large to make the partition. Make the partition as big as possible—the entire disk size, if you can (older versions of DOS may limit how large you can make a partition). DOS will treat each partition as if it were *a separate disk in its own drive* (**C:** , **D:** , **E:**, etc.).

Step 2:   Put the *Install* disk into the **A:** drive. Start the computer, and follow the directions on the screen.... It *may* ask you to switch disks, enter information about your system (printer, keyboard, etc.); or it *may* ask you to choose from certain options. The following options are recommended:

- `Maximum DOS function`
- `Accept predefined keyboard`
- `Install DOS on Drive C:`
- `Install the DOS Shell`
- `Accept Configuration`

Installation takes several minutes. Then go to page 94.

Case 3:   DOS is on a set of disks, *none* of them labelled *Install*. You have no fixed disk (only removable diskettes).

Step 1:   Find the DOS disk labelled *Startup*. If you can't find a disk labelled *Startup,* look for a disk labelled *DOS.* Put this disk into the A: drive and start the computer. If the video screen requests the date and time, enter them.

Step 2:   Create working copies of your *DOS* disks so that if you accidentally change or erase something, you won't ruin your original copies:

  2A: *Format a new, blank disk:*

  Put the startup *DOS* disk into the A: drive.
  At the prompt (A>), type A:\FORMAT A: [←ENTER].
  Follow the directions on the screen.

  2B: *Copy everything from the SOURCE disk (the original) to the TARGET disk (the new copy):*

  Put the startup disk into the A: drive.
  At the A>, type A:\DISKCOPY A: A: [←ENTER].
  Follow the directions on the screen.

  2C: *Label the TARGET disk with the same name as the SOURCE disk.*

Step 3:   **Repeat Step 2** for each disk you need to copy, then go to page 94.

Case 4:   DOS is on a set of disks, *none* of them labelled *Install*. You do have a fixed disk.

Step 1:   Find the DOS disk labelled *Startup*. If you can't find a disk labelled *Startup,* look for one labelled *DOS*. Put this disk into the A: disk drive and start the computer. If the video screen requests the date and time, enter them.

Step 2:   Find out if your fixed disk has been **partitioned**. Partitions logically divide fixed disks into major units. A brand-new fixed disk must be partitioned before it can be used— unless the dealer has done it for you. *If there are files on your fixed disk, it's already partitioned. Partitioning it again will erase those files.*

If your fixed disk is *not* already partitioned:

- Put the startup DOS disk into the A: drive.

- At the prompt (A>), type A:\FDISK ←ENTER.

- Follow the directions on the video screen (if it says that FDISK was not found, put another DOS disk into the drive and try again—you must find the disk with the FDISK command).

- At the A>, type A:\FORMAT C: /S ←ENTER (If you read Chapter 3, you know all about this command—right?)

Step 3:   Make a DOS directory on your fixed disk:

At the **A>**, type **MD C:\DOS** ⟨←ENTER⟩

Step 4:   Copy the DOS files onto the fixed disk:

Leave the DOS disk into the **A:** drive.
At the **A>**, type **COPY A:*.* C:\DOS**
Repeat this for each DOS disk.

Step 5:   Place the **COMMAND.COM** file in the proper directory:

At the **A>**, type **COPY C:\DOS\COMMAND.COM C:**
⟨←ENTER⟩

Protecting Your Original DOS Disks

DOS is installed on your computer system, but you're not finished yet. A lot of possible hazards face your disks: Your dog can chew them up; you might spill coffee on them.; your kids might get jelly on them. And if they survive all that, you may lose them—or wear them out.

Therefore, you should *back up* (i.e., copy) your original DOS disks.* Depending on your version of DOS and the capacities of your disks, you'll have from one to six original disks you should back up.

1: *Format a new, blank disk.*

If you have only removable disks:
> Put the *DOS Startup* disk into the **A:** drive;
> At the **A>**, type **A:\FORMAT A:** (←ENTER); follow directions.

If you have a fixed disk:
> At the **A>**, type **C:\DOS\FORMAT A:** (←ENTER); follow directions.

2: *Copy everything from the* **SOURCE** *disk (the original) to the* **TARGET** *(new) disk.*

If you have only removable disks:
> Put the startup disk into the **A:** drive;
> Enter **A:\DISKCOPY A: A:** and follow the directions.

If you have a fixed disk:
> Enter **C:\DOS\DISKCOPY A: A:** and follow the directions.

3: *Label the* **TARGET** *disk with the same name as the* **SOURCE** *disk.*

Repeat this procedure for each disk you back up.

---

*Even if you've made working copies of your DOS disks, you should still make backups of your original disks!

Preparing Practice Disks

Now prepare the practice disks you'll need during this Easy Course:

- Get four new blank disks and label them: *Power, Power Backup, Boot, Boot Backup.* The *Power* disk will be used to create files and directories and to practice numerous commands. The *Boot disk* will allow you to customize your computer automatically whenever it's turned on. The backups to these disks will teach you how to protect such valuable disk files.

- Format the *Power, Power Backup* and *Boot Backup* disks. Do the following once for each:

  If you have only removable disks: Place the working copy of the DOS *Startup* disk into drive **A:**. At the **A>**, type **A:\FORMAT A:** (←ENTER), and follow directions. If the screen asks you to name volume labels, enter **EASYCOURSE**.

  For a fixed disk: At the **A>**, type **C:\DOS\FORMAT A:** (←ENTER)

- Format the *Boot* disk—using the **/S** switch (recall page 82):

  If you have only removable disks: Place the working copy of the DOS *Startup* disk into the **A:** drive. At the **A>**, type **A:\FORMAT A: /S** (←ENTER), and follow directions. If you're asked to name volume labels, enter **BOOT**.

  Fixed disk: At the **A>**, type **C:\DOS\FORMAT A: /S** (←ENTER).

Now your practice disks are ready for action...

5. BOOT CAMP

The "Boot" Process

*Ten-**hut**!* This is your basic training in DOS. You'll hear the word "boot" a lot around computers, so you might as well know about it: When the computer is turned on, it is *booted*. That is, your computer is "pulling itself up by its own bootstraps."

Sound strange? The reasons for this term become a lot clearer if you follow what the computer actually does when you flip on that power switch—it literally loads and tests itself!...

Step 1: *The ROM Chip* Stored permanently on a ROM chip inside the computer are the very first instructions the computer sees when it "wakes up." Essentially, this code directs the computer to "Start Here."

Step 2: *The Self-Test* The next instructions on that ROM chip tell the computer to perform a **Power-On** Self Test (**POST**)—to make sure that it's all there and ready for action.

This POST self-diagnosis is most obvious to you when it's testing the RAM, because the computer displays the checked-kilobyte count (e.g. a computer with 640 kilobytes of memory will count up to 640 on the display when it boots). This is actually a *humongous* task. As you know, 640K = 655,360 bytes = 5,242,880 bits. So if you get impatient waiting the few seconds for your computer to test its 640K of RAM, remember that that's over five million bits!

Step 3: *The Boot Record*   After the POST, the final instructions on the ROM tell the machine to find and load into memory a ***boot record***, or ***boot sector***, *from a disk*—any disk available (its search pattern starts with the **A :** drive, then on to the fixed disk, **C :** , if one is present). In this search, the computer doesn't look for any directories or filenames. It seeks only the very *first* sector—the boot sector—on the disk. The ROM's instructions load this record into the computer's memory (RAM) and *then the loaded boot record begins to issue the commands.*

Step 4: ***IO . SYS***   The boot record loads the **IO . SYS** file (if it can find it on the disk) into the computer's memory *and turns control over to it.* **IO . SYS** then begins to run the BIOS (Basic Input/Output Services) to manage the details of the input and output devices of your machine.

Step 5: ***MSDOS . SYS***   Next, the **IO . SYS** file loads the **MSDOS . SYS** file into memory and turns over control to it. **MSDOS . SYS** is the *kernel* (or "colonel") program which handles the low-level details for running your system: allocating memory for other programs, loading them and running them, etc.

Step 6: ***CONFIG . SYS***   After the **MSDOS . SYS** file itself ("DOS") is loaded in the boot process, it checks for a **CONFIG . SYS** file on the disk. If there is one, then DOS reads the information in the **CONFIG . SYS** file to learn about and *configure* the machine's settings and devices.

Step 7: COMMAND.COM   Although the real "make-it-happen" DOS file is **MSDOS.SYS**, it's not easy for humans to communicate with—because it's running *machine code* (recall page 46). So DOS actually loads another file to allow you to communicate with it. That "spokesman" or interpreter file is **COMMAND.COM**.

Because it acts in this vital interpretive role, **COMMAND.COM** is also called a *user interface* or *shell*, because it provides a way that you, the user, can interface with the computer—you "see" the computer because you see this shell. Thus, **COMMAND.COM** is the file that has been the visible part of DOS for so many years—the program you "speak to" whenever you type at the DOS "ready" prompt (**A>**).

Step 8: *Time and Date*   The boot process isn't finished yet, though: When you wake up, you usually check the time, right? So does your computer. It has a very accurate timing chip to coordinate the running of programs, and it uses this to keep a normal, chronological clock, too. But when the machine is off, the timer doesn't operate—and so the computer has no way of resetting its clock

To remedy this, some computers use a rechargeable battery to keep enough current for a *built-in* clock. Otherwise, DOS simply asks *you* for the date and time each time it boots. If you don't want to bother with entering the correct date and time, just press ENTER, and the request will be skipped.

Step 9: *AUTOEXEC.BAT*   Next, DOS looks for the **AUTOEXEC.BAT** file, a specially-named *batch file*—a set of DOS commands (the kind you normally type at the **A>**) that run here *automatically*. This is one good way you can further customize your system for your convenience: You put commands into this **AUTOEXEC.BAT** file, so that your computer executes them automatically each time it boots.

Step 10:   *The DOS Shell (Version 4.00 and greater)*   Although **COMMAND.COM** does interpret usable DOS commands for the underlying DOS kernel (the **MSDOS.SYS** file), many users have found even those interpreted commands to be a bit cryptic and inconvenient.

So the DOS Shell* is an attempt to improve that situation. The DOS Shell doesn't replace **COMMAND.COM**; rather, it can be generated *from* it (and you'll soon see how).

Well, then *why* (you might ask) should you have to learn to type the DOS commands at the **A>** for the **COMMAND.COM** interpreter if you have the friendlier DOS Shell available to you?

It's because the DOS Shell can't do everything. That's why it still allows you to exit to the DOS prompt (**A>**). The Shell can make things easier for you, but it doesn't replace the knowledge you need to best manage your computer. It's like a frosted window: It has nice visual look, but it also blocks much of your vision of what's going on inside.

---

*Since **COMMAND.COM** is the first layer of shell for the **MSDOS.SYS** kernel, the DOS Shell is actually a *second-level* shell. But now everyone simply calls it "the" Shell. Don't let this throw you.

Types of Boots

So *that's* what happens when you boot the computer. You can see how it is a boot-strapping process, no? *Each file or instruction set loads the next set, then turns over control to those newly-loaded instructions.*

But just how do you *do* this boot?

1. Just turn on your computer. This is called a *hard boot*. You know that when you turn off the computer, you lose any information in the computer's memory (but not what's stored on a disk).

2. Press `CTRL`-`ALT`-`DEL`—all three keys *simultaneously*. This is called a *soft boot* or a *reset*. When you soft boot, the computer also loses its memory, just as if you turned off the machine.

3. Some computers have a special reset button, which simply does the same thing as `CTRL`-`ALT`-`DEL`.

4. Some applications programs (e.g. word processors, spreadsheets, games, etc.) are called *self booting*, because they have **IO.SYS**, **MSDOS.SYS**, and **COMMAND.COM** on the same disk as the applications program. So you don't have to insert the DOS startup disk first—you can just insert the program disk: Put the one disk in; turn on the computer—what could be easier?* The computer still goes through the self diagnostics, but then it goes straight into the game or spreadsheet, or whatever.

---

*However, these programs cannot be installed on fixed disks. Also, as computers become more sophisticated, they can "multi-task"—run more than one program at once—and self-booting programs can't be used in that way.

Making a Simple Boot Disk

You now have the expertise necessary to make a simple boot disk.

Question: What's the difference between a *Startup* disk and a *Boot* disk?

Answer: A *Startup* disk is one of the "store-bought" DOS disks you can use to start the computer the "vanilla" way. A *Boot* disk is a disk you customize to start the computer in "flavors" more to your liking.

Both startup disks and boot disks **require** these three files to get DOS up and running:

- **IO.SYS**,
- **MSDOS.SYS**
- **COMMAND.COM**

When you format a disk with the **/S** switch, these three files are put onto the disk—and you did just that with the *Boot* disk in the previous chapter.

So you're off to a good start—but you're not finished, yet. You have a *Boot* disk, but it's not customized. To customize it, you may include—and alter—two more files:

- **CONFIG.SYS**
- **AUTOEXEC.BAT**

To get you a feel for how that might work—and to help make DOS much more convenient—here's a necessary example. Even if you don't fully understand what's going on here, go through these keystrokes anyway. You'll be glad you did—and understand why—a little later....

Do This: Create an **AUTOEXEC.BAT** file on your *Boot* Disk which will make external commands appear to be internal.

Like So: Put your *Boot Disk* into the **A:** drive. Then:

> *Type:* **TYPE CON > A:\AUTOEXEC.BAT** (←ENTER)
> *Type*:* **PATH C:\DOS** (←ENTER)
> *Type:* (F6) (←ENTER)

Things will now be much more convenient for you when working with a fixed disk. Previously, you had to type **C:\DOS\FORMAT** in order to tell DOS to look for the **FORMAT** command in the **C:\DOS** path (recall the discussion on pages 77-81). But now you can simply type **FORMAT** and DOS will know enough to automatically look in right place.

However, an **AUTOEXEC.BAT** file doesn't go into effect until the computer is booted with it. So leave the *Boot Disk* in the **A** drive and reboot the computer now.

---

*If you don't have a fixed disk, type **PATH A:\DOS** (←ENTER) for this line.

Notes (Yours)

Bootiful Questions

1. How do you boot your computer?

2. Why is it called a "boot"?

3. When are the components of a computer tested?

4. Describe the steps of a boot.

5. What's the difference between a hard boot and a soft boot?

6. What's the difference between **COMMAND.COM**, which is a shell, and the *DOS Shell*, which is also a shell?

7. What's a default path?

Dutiful Answers

1. Make sure that the computer has access (in one of the disk drives) to a DOS *Startup* disk or a *Boot* disk. Then, either:

   - turn the computer on; or
   - simultaneously press the `CTRL`-`ALT`-`DEL` keys; or
   - push the *reset* button if your machine has one.

2. It's because the computer "pulls itself up by its own bootstraps." That is, it sequentially loads increasingly sophisticated instructions into memory, then runs those instructions.

3. The machine does a **Power-On** Self Test (POST) whenever it boots.

4. 1. A ROM chip in the computer starts the process.
    2. The ROM performs a Power-On Self Test (POST).
    3. The ROM loads the *boot record* from a disk.
    4. The boot record loads the **IO.SYS** file from the disk.
    5. The **IO.SYS** file activates the machine's I/O functions and then loads the actual DOS "kernel" program—**MSDOS.SYS**.
    6. DOS obtains the settings in the **CONFIG.SYS** file, if any.
    7. DOS loads the **COMMAND.COM** program to act as a *shell*, or interpreter, for interfacing (communicating) with you.
    8. DOS obtains the date and time.
    9. DOS performs any commands in the **AUTOEXEC.BAT** file.
    10. DOS runs the DOS Shell program (if it has been installed).

5. You perform a hard boot when you turn the computer on—also called a cold boot because the computer is off and "cold" at the time. To do a soft boot, you press `CTRL`-`ALT`-`DEL` (all keys at the same time) or press a reset button (not all machines have one of these). A soft boot is also called a *warm boot* because the computer is already on and "warm."

6. They are both shells in that they are the "interpreters" of DOS that you actually see. **COMMAND.COM** is the more primitive ("lower-level")—and therefore the more powerful—of the two shells, because it "wraps around" the DOS kernel (**MSDOS.SYS**) program itself, interpreting the specific DOS commands and options that you type in at the DOS prompt (**A>**).

    The DOS Shell is a *second-level* shell: It actually wraps around the **COMMAND.COM** shell, making that easier to understand ("friendlier") by making most (but not all) of its interpretations of DOS available through pre-set *menus*—rather than the more cryptic (but more powerful) **A>** commands of **COMMAND.COM**

7. A *default* path is the path which DOS uses to find a file *when you don't specify any other* (recall pages 77-81). Remember that you can specify any path you wish in the pathname(s) of a command's parameter(s); when you don't, DOS uses the default path. As you saw (without explanation yet), you can *supplement* this default path with the **PATH** command—and even automate its execution by putting it into the **AUTOEXEC.BAT** file, which is read and executed every time you boot the computer.

6. PROMPTS AND SHELLS

The DOS Prompt

As you may know by now, the DOS prompt is the little message that signals to you that the machine is waiting for your next instruction. The basic idea is: You tell it to do something—say, run an applications program; it does it, and then it comes back and prompts you for the next instruction.* Here are the typical DOS prompts:

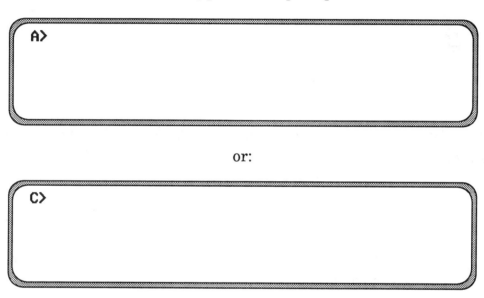

```
A>
```

or:

```
C>
```

These are the "normal" prompts. The **A** or the **C** in the prompt tells you immediately which disk drive is currently in use, because in *DOS*, disk drives are named with letters of the alphabet.

If you have only floppy disk drives in your system, then the prompt is usually **A>** (a single floppy drive is named the **A:** drive; a dual-floppy system normally has **A:** and **B:** drives). If you have a fixed disk in your system, it's usually in the **C:** drive.

*Some applications programs aren't that well designed: They don't leave you back at the prompt when they finish; you must *reboot* the computer—just to get the DOS prompt back!

This business of naming disk drives isn't exactly rocket science: the names for the drives simply proceed right through the alphabet. If you were to add more disk drives to your system, they'd be the **D** drive, the **E** drive, etc.. So any of these prompts is also possible (but you'll see only one at a time):

```
D>
E>
F>
G>
```

The letter in the prompt simply indicates which disk drive is currently being used.

That's all there is to it.

As for the **>** , it's simply used as a pointer—as if the **A>** prompt was really giving you the message:

```
I'm now using the A disk drive and awaiting your
next command.  Put it right here>
```

That's a more explicit prompt.

Responding to the DOS Prompt

So the DOS prompt is asking you for a command. Guess you'd better give it one. Here are you choices:

- You can give a DOS *command*—something you tell the system to do or change. For example, you can tell it to change which disk drive it's using—from A to C, for instance.

    Commands are specific words known to DOS. As you know, some are "built-in" (*internal* commands). Others require a DOS disk to be present (*external* commands).

- You can give it a *keyword* to begin an applications program. A keyword is simply the name of the file containing the applications program. When you type the keyword, this simply tells DOS to find that program file and run it.

No matter what you want to do, you have to know the proper *command* or *keyword*—and how to respond to the DOS prompt. So get ready to practice now with the prompt:

- Make sure that you have booted your computer with your *Boot* disk in the A: drive.

- And if you're in the DOS Shell, press F3 now, to exit it.

Changing the DOS Prompt

First, try an internal command: Tell DOS to change which disk drive it reads and writes (provided, of course, that you have at least two disk drives). For example, if you have an **A:** drive (for floppy disks) and a **C:** drive (for a fixed disk), sometimes you'll want to change which one you're using....

Challenge: Suppose the DOS prompt is telling you that the system is currently using fixed disk **C**, like this:

```
C>
```

Command it to change to floppy disk drive **A**.

Solution: Type **A:**. The screen will look like this:

```
C>A:
```

Now press [←ENTER], *to signal the end of the instruction.* Instantly you'll see the new prompt:

```
A>
```

To get back to the **C:** drive (the fixed disk) once again, just type **C:** and press [←ENTER]. Nothing to it!

Who Wants to Be Normal?

Rumor has it that it's entirely possible to make the DOS prompt appear radically different than the boring old **A>** or **C>**. It's true: There's a DOS command, called **PROMPT**, that lets you _customize_ the DOS prompt.

Try It: Make sure that you're seeing some kind of DOS prompt—probably **A>** or **C>**. Now, type:

PROMPT What is your command, O master?

and press ⌊←ENTER⌋....

Result:

> **What is your command, O master?**

That's more _like_ it, eh?

You can make the DOS prompt say anything you want! All you do is type **PROMPT**, then your customized prompt message, then ⌊←ENTER⌋.

Great, huh? And you can always return to the standard prompt by typing **PROMPT** (with nothing else) and ⌊←ENTER⌋.*

But there's even more you can do with the **PROMPT** command....

*To signal the end of an instruction, you must always press ⌊←ENTER⌋. (Note that the ⌊←ENTER⌋ key is sometimes called ⌊ENTER⌋ or ⌊RETURN⌋ or ⌊CARRIAGE RETURN⌋ or something similar.)

PROMPT and $

DOS has some special features which you can include in your customized prompt by using the $ symbol in just the right way. For example, if you want your customized prompt to show the current time, you could use the old $t trick.

Go for It: Type: **PROMPT It is now $t. More or less.**
Press (←ENTER).

Result: The computer will put its current clock time *in place of* the $t. Thus, you'll see something like the following (the actual time shown will be different):

> It is now 06:47:29.34.   More or less.

The dollar sign used within a **PROMPT** command directs the computer to replace the $ and its code letter with something.

Besides the time, there are many other things the **PROMPT** command can look up and include in your customized prompt (see Appendix C on page 332 for a complete list):

$d   looks up the current date.
$v   looks up the current version number of your DOS software.
$n   looks up the "letter" of the disk drive currently being used.
$_   continues your prompt on the next line.

Isn't it amazing what you can do with a dollar sign?*

Earlier you merely "humbled" your computer. Now, knowing all this, you can make it long-winded —or give it an attitude—if you want....

Try This: Type in the following prompt. It's probably longer than the width of your screen, but just keep typing—don't press ◄─ENTER until you finish the entire command:

```
PROMPT The date is $d$_The time is
$t$_The operating system is $v$_The
current disk drive is $n$_So whaddya
want, Bitbrain?$_
```

Result: (Something similar to this):

```
The date is Mon 2-05-1990
The time is 11:04:57.82
The operating system is MS-DOS Version 4.01
The current disk drive is A
So whaddya want, Bitbrain?
```

Talk about a "personalized" prompt! (Feel free to change this any way you want—or back to the standard prompt.)

---

*But you probably learned that long ago, right?

The DOS Shell

There's a problem with DOS's prompt-level *shell* (the **COMMAND.COM** program that reads your typed commands and translates them for the machine-level DOS kernel): It takes a lot of memorization to type the commands. Obviously, if you don't know what the commands are, you can't use them.

So now you have *second-level* shells—to make the DOS commands more friendly—usually by hiding them behind easier-to-use *menus*. The most sophisticated type of this second-level menu-driven shell is a *GUI* ("gooey")—a **G**raphical **U**ser **I**nterface (**GUI**). This just means it uses graphics, usually in the form of *icons*, or small pictures.

The DOS Shell, available with DOS Version 4.00 and later, is somewhat like a gooey. To use its graphics advantages fully, you need to have a fixed disk and (preferably) a mouse.

So, does the *DOS Shell*, with its convenient menus, completely replace the DOS prompt—and the need for you to learn about that prompt?

No!

The *DOS Shell* can't do everything. In fact, there are about five different ways to *exit* the shell—to get back to the DOS prompt. So obviously, Microsoft acknowledges that you'll often want to do this.

Program Shells

Some applications programs (e.g. word processors, spreadsheets, games, etc.) also have DOS-prompt shells. That is, these programs allow you access to a DOS prompt—to type DOS commands—*without leaving those programs.* Here's how such a program would work:

- **COMMAND.COM** is loaded into memory at boot time.

- You enter the keyword and DOS loads the application program (say, a word processor) into memory and begins running it.

- This word processor program "calls" the **COMMAND.COM** shell.

- A *fresh copy* of **COMMAND.COM** is then loaded into memory (so **COMMAND.COM** is now in memory twice)!

- Since you're now seeing a DOS prompt, you do whatever DOS commands you want. When you enter the DOS **EXIT** command, this second copy of the **COMMAND.COM** shell is exited—and erased from memory. Control of the computer then returns to the word processor program.

- When *that* program is exited, control returns to the first copy of **COMMAND.COM**—which is still in memory.

So program shells add multiple layers of shell on top of the original **COMMAND.COM** shell that is loaded at boot time. You can enter the applications program, enter the **COMMAND.COM** shell, enter the program again, enter the **COMMAND.COM** shell, again, and keep going like this—until you run out of memory!

Learning the Shell Game

As you can tell, sometimes, it's tough to keep track of what shell contains what! But now that you have some understanding of different types of shells, you can at least compare them to see how they're alike (and different).

- **COMMAND.COM**

    This is the original (first-level) shell which contains the DOS prompt and interprets your typed DOS commands.

- Program shells

    These are just instances of where an applications program calls a fresh copy of the **COMMAND.COM** shell as a sub-routine—to give you access to the *DOS* prompt without leaving the applications program.

- The DOS Shell

    This is the name of a particular *second-level* shell. That is, it "wraps around" and interprets most of **COMMAND.COM** through *menus*. This program is distributed with DOS in versions 4.00 and greater.

- Other *second-level* shells

    These are other programs which invoke most of **COMMAND.COM** through menus. Many varieties are available, including Graphical User Interfaces (GUI's) which use graphical menus to invoke some *DOS* commands.

Prompt Inquiries

1. What does the standard DOS prompt look like?

2. How do you instruct DOS to change the current (default) disk drive?

3. What can you enter from the DOS prompt?

4. What's the difference between the DOS prompt and the DOS Shell?

5. Can shells perform all of the DOS commands?

6. How would you change the DOS prompt to display this?

   ## At your service...

   And then how would you change it back to the standard prompt?

7. Suppose you have a word processor that has a DOS shell. How would you load both the word processor and a game program at the same time? How many programs would this put into memory at the same time?

Prompt Responses

1. The standard DOS prompt is **A>** or **C>**, depending upon whether the **A:** drive or the **C:** drive is currently in use (i.e. the default).

2. You enter the new disk drive with a colon. For example, to change from the **A:** drive to the **C:** drive, you'd type **C:** ⌨ENTER.

3. You can enter a DOS command or a keyword. Since external DOS commands are individual programs, those commands are really keywords—just like those of applications programs.

4. The DOS prompt requires that you type in commands; the DOS Shell offers you menus to select commands.

5. Shells can perform only some of the available commands. That's why they must give you ways to return to the DOS prompt.

6. Type: **PROMPT At your service...** ⌨ENTER.

   To change it back, just type **PROMPT** ⌨ENTER.

7. You can run any number of programs with shells—until memory fills up. First, you would run the word processor. Then, within that program you would use whatever command it offered you to invoke the shell. That would give you access to a DOS prompt, so then you would enter the keyword to start the game program. At least six programs would then be in memory at once:

- **IO.SYS** (loaded at boot time)

- **MSDOS.SYS** (loaded at boot time)

- The first copy of **COMMAND.COM** (loaded at boot time)

- The word processor (loaded when you typed its keyword at the DOS prompt of the first copy of **COMMAND.COM**)

- The second copy of **COMMAND.COM** (loaded when you selected that as an option offered by the word processor)

- The game (loaded when you typed its keyword at the DOS prompt of the second copy of **COMMAND.COM**)

To get back to the word processor, you would finish the game program. This would return you to the DOS prompt of the *second* **COMMAND.COM**. There you would enter the **EXIT** command, and that second copy of **COMMAND.COM** would be exited and erased, and you would return to the word processor. Four programs would then be in memory:

- **IO.SYS**
- **MSDOS.SYS**
- The first copy of **COMMAND.COM**
- The word processor

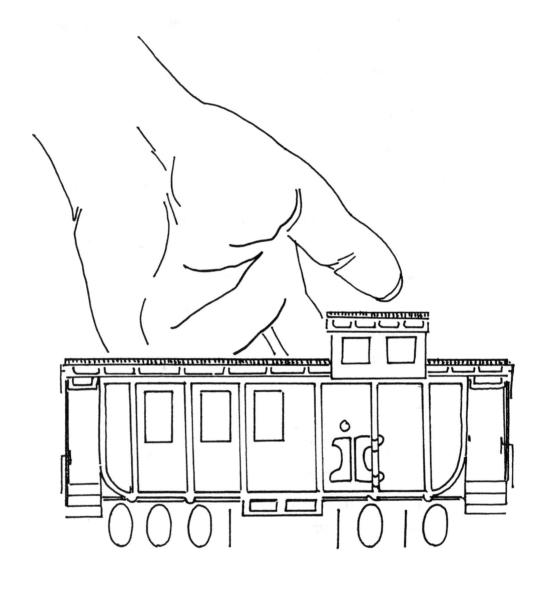

7. MAKING AND STORING TEXT FILES

Types of Files

Before you can do anything with files, you'd better know a few things about files in general.

First of all, there are basically three types of files that DOS can handle:

- **Program files** contain program code which can be run by the computer. These files are created by an assembler, a compiler, or an interpreter (recall pages 46-48).

- **Data files** contain information coded in bytes which can be used by programs to represent and store information (data). The meaning of the bytes in a data file *depends on the program that created them;* they mean what that program *says* they mean.

- **Text files** contain bytes representing characters according to the **ASCII** code (recall pages 25 and 69). Some text files are in pure **ASCII** code and therefore can be utilized by a wide variety of programs. Other "text" files have non-text data bytes mixed in with the characters.

This chapter will show you how to use DOS to create pure **ASCII** text files. And in the process, you'll start to learn how files are stored in directories....

Making Text Files With **TYPE**

Actually, you've already created a text file—that **AUTOEXEC.BAT** file you put onto your *Boot* disk back on page 103. But now it's time to take a closer look at the **TYPE** command you used then.

TYPE is an internal command; you don't have to enter a disk drive identifier or a pathname before the **TYPE** command, because it's already in memory—within the **COMMAND.COM** program.

TYPE can tell DOS to perform a variety of *typing* functions—putting text characters someplace. For example, it can:

- type your keystrokes from the keyboard into a file on a disk;
- type your keystrokes from the keyboard directly to a printer;
- type the contents of a file onto the screen.

Start with the first of these functions—typing your keystrokes to a file: Put the *Boot* disk into the **A:** drive and boot your computer. Then, at the DOS prompt, take out the *Boot* disk and insert the *Power* disk. **A:** will be the default drive (the prompt will be **A>**). Now then:

Challenge: Create a file containing a telephone number.

Solution: *Type:* **TYPE CON > PHONE.TXT** ⎡←ENTER⎤
      Grapevine 1-800-338-4331 ⎡←ENTER⎤
      ⎡F6⎤⎡←ENTER⎤

Challenge: Create a file containing an address.

Solution: *Type:* **TYPE CON > ADDRESS.TXT** (←ENTER)
        Grapevine Publications, Inc. (←ENTER)
        P.O. Box 2449 (←ENTER)
        Corvallis, OR 97339 (←ENTER)
        (F6)(←ENTER)

Challenge: Make a file of things to do.

Solution: *Type:* **TYPE CON > TODO.TXT** (←ENTER)
        1. Take out the garbage. (←ENTER)
        2. Wash the dishes. (←ENTER)
        3. Call Josie. (←ENTER)
        (F6)(←ENTER)

See the pattern here? Each solution consists of three steps:

1. Identify the file to which you want to type;

2. Enter the text itself;

3. Enter (F6) to indicate the end of the file.

Displaying Files

You've probably noticed something else, too—that word **CON** (short for **CON**sole). This has a special meaning to DOS: The _console_ is the _keyboard_ for input (e.g. typing a file), but it's the _monitor_ for output (e.g. displaying a file). So this command sentence:

TYPE CON > TODO.TXT

says "type _from_ the **con**sole (keyboard) _to_ the **TODO.TXT** file."

Try This: _Type:_ **TYPE TODO.TXT > CON** [←ENTER]

Result: The **TODO.TXT** file appears on the screen, right? This time, something is being typed _to_ (>) **CON**, so this would be the output **CON**—the monitor screen.

Actually, it's so common to want to do this that the DOS default for **TYPE** is > **CON**—so you can leave it out:

```
TYPE TODO.TXT    = TYPE TODO.TXT > CON
TYPE PHONE.TXT   = TYPE PHONE.TXT > CON
TYPE ADDRESS.TXT = TYPE ADDRESS.TXT > CON
```

Do This: Display the **AUTOEXEC.BAT** file.

Like So: Put your _Boot_ disk into the **A:** drive and type:
                  TYPE AUTOEXEC.BAT [←ENTER]

Using the **EDLIN** Program

As you've no doubt found out by now, the **TYPE** command has a serious drawback when creating text files: You can't make corrections or changes. So now try **EDLIN**, an external DOS *command* that acts as a *line editor*—a quick-and-dirty word processor.

First: Put **EDLIN** onto your *Power* disk:

If you have a *fixed disk*, put your *Power* disk into the **A:** drive and type **COPY C:\DOS\EDLIN.* A:** ⟨←ENTER⟩.

If you have only *removable disks:* Put any DOS working disk into the **A:** drive. If you have a **B:** drive, put the *Power* disk in there.* If not, DOS will tell you when to put it into the **A:** drive. Type **COPY A:EDLIN.* B:** ⟨←ENTER⟩.**

---

*If your two removable disk drives are of different sizes, then, of course, your *Power* disk won't fit into the **B:** drive. In general, then, *anytime* you want to copy a file between two disks of the same size, you're going to need to do an extra step. To prepare for this extra step, put the DOS *Startup* disk into the **A:** drive and a blank, unformatted disk into the **B:** drive. Type **A:\FORMAT B:** ⟨←ENTER⟩. Label the newly-formatted disk *Ferry*, since that will be its role.

Then, for example, to copy the **EDLIN** file to the *Power* disk (which is the point of the above exercise), you put the disk containing **EDLIN** into the **A:** drive and the *Ferry* disk into the **B:** drive, and type **COPY A:EDLIN.* B:** ⟨←ENTER⟩. That's the extra step. Then you put the *Power* disk into the **A:** drive and type **COPY B:\EDLIN.* A:** ⟨←ENTER⟩.

If you get a **File not found message, just try different DOS working disks in drive **A:** until you find the disk containing **EDLIN**. This is a clumsy way to find a file on a disk (you'll soon learn a better way), but it does show that there's usually more than one way to do things in DOS—and that there's no need to panic when you see a **File not found** message.

Making Text Files with EDLIN*

The **EDLIN** *prompt* is a *****. The common commands spell **IDLE**:

I = Insert line(s);   **D** = Delete line(s);   **L** = List line(s);   **E** = End

---

Challenge: Use **EDLIN** to create a shopping list on the *Power* disk.

Solution: Make sure the *Power* disk is in the **A:** drive. Then type:

EDLIN SHOP.TXT (←ENTER) (you see the ***** prompt)
I (←ENTER)   (you see line 1)
Milk (←ENTER) **Bread** (←ENTER) **Eggs** (←ENTER)
(F6) (←ENTER)   (marks the end of the file)
E (←ENTER)   (ends the editing; saves the file on disk)

Now: Use **EDLIN** to write a memo announcing a meeting.

Easy: Type (and press (←ENTER) at the end of each line):

EDLIN MEMO.TXT
I
Strange Brew Computer Club will meet
Wednesday at 6 p.m. in the lounge.
(F6)
E

Get the idea? Now use **TYPE** to see your handiwork.

---

*If you're using DOS version 5.0, you should be aware that it offers a command called **EDIT**, which far outshines **EDLIN** (though it's still good to know **EDLIN**). To start **EDIT** from a fixed drive, just enter **EDIT**. To start it from a removable drive, put the DOS *Basic/Edit* disk into the **A:** drive and enter **A:\EDIT**. The instructions ("Survival Guide") for **EDIT** are built into the command.

Editing Text Files

So far, what you've done with **EDLIN** could also be done with **TYPE** (if you type carefully). But now here's the Big Difference....

Can You: Take bread off the shopping list and add ham?

Sure: Everything in **EDLIN** is oriented toward _lines_ of text— all lines are numbered. For example, **5,10D** means "delete lines 5 through 10." So, to amend your shopping list, just _type_ (and press (←ENTER) after each line):

EDLIN SHOP.TXT	(gets the file)
L	(Lists the file contents)
2D	(Deletes Line 2)
3I	(prepares to Insert on Line 3)
Ham	(the new Line 3)
(F6)	(marks the end of the file)
E	(ends the session/saves the file)

Can You: Change the computer club meeting time to 7 p.m.?

Yep: _Type_ (and press (←ENTER) at the end of each line):

EDLIN MEMO.TXT	(gets the file)
L	(Lists—displays—the file)
2	(the line number to edit)
Wednesday at 7 p.m. in the lounge.	
	(you must replace _the entire line_)
E	(ends the session/saves the file)

More About Text Files

The Caboose Byte

In all these examples you've been pressing F6 without really understanding what this important key does.

As you know, words and sentences are stored in a computer file—a text file—as a series of bytes. Imagine a byte as being a railroad car with eight wheels—eight bits. Just as a railroad car carries cargo, a byte carries information. Well, there must be one particular byte to act as the caboose of this "train"—so that DOS can detect when the end of a file has been reached.

That byte is 00011010, which has a decimal value of 26 and is the **ASCII** code for the character *"control-Z"* (CTRL Z)—designated on the screen by **^Z**. In fact, you probably observed that F6 in the previous examples produced a **^Z** on the screen.

This was to enter the all-important caboose byte—to tell DOS's **TYPE** and **EDLIN** commands that you were at the end of your text file. *You could have done it yourself,* by literally pressing CTRL Z (holding down the CTRL key while pressing Z), but the F6 key was easier.

In sum:

$$00011010 = \text{decimal } 26 = \text{CTRL } \text{Z} = {}^{}\!Z = \text{F6}$$

= *the caboose byte*—called the **End Of File** (**EOF**) marker
in official computer jargon.

The Root Directory

Stop and consider this for a moment: You've been busily typing files onto your *Power* disk—but where exactly have they been going? It's time to look at this now....

Since you didn't specify anywhere in particular, your files went onto the disk in the default drive (that was drive A:), where your *Power* disk was. And since there was only one directory on that disk, your first text files went into it—the *root directory*.

You read a little bit about the root directory back on page 79, but here's a reminder: A **directory** is a portion of a disk which you set aside to contain certain files. Unlike tracks, sectors, and clusters, which have physical locations on a disk, directories are very flexible: They can be large or small, their files can be scattered all over the place on the disk—and they can come and go. So DOS needs some way to keep track of them. It does this with the **root directory**, which keeps a list of all other directories.

Of course, a root directory can contain *files* as well as the other directories. Indeed, most floppy disks usually have all their files in the root directory—because there's not room for enough files to demand other directories. But the crucial, unique role of a root directory is to keep track of all the other directories on the disk.

One more thing: With several directories on a disk, you must instruct DOS where to find them. You do this with **pathnames** (remember these—pages 77-81?). In a pathname, the directory specifiers are separated by backslashes (\). And the *shortest* pathname is a single backslash, which means "no path"—i.e. the root directory itself.

Erasing Files

What goes up must come down ... and whatever files you make you must be able to delete. DOS provides two commands to erase files. One is **DEL** (**DEL**ete) and the other is **ERASE**.

Do It: Delete (erase) the **MEMO.TXT** file from your *Power* disk in the **A:** drive.

Like This: *Type:* **DEL MEMO.TXT** [←ENTER]

Or This: *Type:* **ERASE MEMO.TXT** [←ENTER]

Both **DEL** and **ERASE** are internal commands, so you don't have to find them on a disk in order to invoke them. Choose either one of them when you need to erase a file.

DOS does more than just let you make and delete files in the root directory. One of the biggest challenges is to organize your disk space so that files can be efficiently located and managed. All that's coming up next, but first...

Check Yourself

1. Of the three types of files, which type do **TYPE** and **EDLIN** make?

2. What's a directory? What's the difference between the *root* directory and any other directory?

3. Use **EDLIN** to add "**Sara 1-555-1212**" and "**John 1-555-2121**" to the phone file.

4. What's the Big Difference between **EDLIN** and **TYPE**?

5. Why might you say that the **CON**sole has a split personality?

6. How would you create—and then view—the following memo?

    ```
    John,

    A manager's meeting will be held at the Holiday
    Motel next Tuesday at 7:00 p.m.

    Bring the Harleystead Contract.

        The Boss
    ```

7. What if you already have a file named **MEMO.TXT** and you want to make another one?

How Did You Do?

1. The three types of files are program files, data files, and text files. **TYPE** and **EDLIN** make *text* files.

2. A directory is a dynamic file organizer on a disk. It keeps track of the files and the other directories ("subdirectories") it contains. Directories can grow and shrink and come and go—you create and name them. However, every disk has a root directory— the first one on the disk—from which all other directories grow.

    When specifying pathnames within a directory structure, the backslash precedes a directory name. A lone \ means "no path" —i.e. the root directory:

    \ means the root directory of the disk in the default drive.

    A:** means the root directory of the disk in the **A: drive.

    A:\MEMO.TXT means the **MEMO.TXT** file in the root directory of the disk in the **A:** drive.

3. Put the *Power* disk into the **A:** drive, and type these lines (ending each line with ⌫ENTER):

    ```
    EDLIN PHONE.TXT
    2I
    Sara 1-555-1212
    John 1-555 2121
    ```
    F6
    ```
    E
    ```

    (To see the changes, enter **TYPE PHONE.TXT**.)

4. **EDLIN** can *edit* text files; **TYPE** can't.

5. The word **CON**sole can denote either of two different *devices,* depending upon how it's used: For input, **CON** is the keyboard; for output, **CON** is the monitor.

6. *Type:* **EDLIN JOHN.TXT** (←ENTER), to establish the file.

    I (←ENTER)

    (Line 1 will appear and you can enter your memo, including extra (←ENTER)'s for blank lines)

    (F6)(←ENTER)
    E (←ENTER)

    To view the resulting file, type: **TYPE JOHN.TXT** (←ENTER).

7. Here's the problem: If you use the **TYPE** command, the second **MEMO.TXT** file will *overwrite* the first one.

    If you use **EDLIN**, the first file will be recalled and you can't start a second file. You can overcome these hurdles in the next chapter, where, by properly organizing a disk, several files of the *same name* can co-exist.

8. ORGANIZING AND FINDING YOUR FILES

Directories and DIR

Computer disks save files in directory *trees*. And the better you nurture your trees, the better you'll be able to organize and find your files. You'll learn all about trees in this chapter—but first, you need to know more about directories.

Without the DIRectory command, your disk drive is like a black box: Information goes in and information comes out, but you don't know exactly what's in the box. Some people use their disks that way. They don't know for sure what's there, and finding programs and files is largely guesswork.

Naturally, there's a better way—the DIRectory command. It's like a TV camera aimed at your disk: you can see the results on your video when you use the DIR command to:

- locate a program or other file on one of several disks;

- check on the amount of disk space you have left;

- verify your file movements and other file management activities;

As you might guess, you'll probably use the DIR command more than any other DOS command—because it gives you such a useful view of the action....

The DIR Command

Boot your computer with the *Boot* disk.... Then put the *Power* disk into the A: drive and type **DIR** ⎯ENTER (**DIR** is an *internal* command—no need for a pathname to help DOS find it). You'll see something like this:

```
Volume in drive A is EASYCOURSE
Volume Serial Number is 0E56-12E0
Directory of A:\

PHONE     BAK        26   01-01-80    12:01a
ADDRESS   TXT        98   01-01-80    12:02a
TODO      TXT        66   01-01-80    12:03a
EDLIN     COM     14069   11-30-88    12:00a
SHOP      BAK        20   02-24-90     8:14p
MEMO      BAK        85   02-24-90     8:15p
PHONE     TXT        61   02-24-90     8:30p
SHOP      TXT        18   02-24-90     8:20p
JOHN      TXT       170   02-24-90     8:32p
        9 File(s)      339968 bytes free
```

This is a **DIR***ectory listing*. Notice these things about it:

- The *volume label:* "**Volume in drive A is EASYCOURSE**"
  This is the identifying name you've given to the disk—in this case, **EASYCOURSE**.

- The *volume serial #:* "**Volume Serial Number is 0E56-12E0**"
  This is an identifying random number assigned to the disk.

- The *specified directory:* "**Directory of A:**"
  A disk often has multiple directories. This says which directory is being listed—here, the *root* directory of the disk in the A: drive.

- The *list of files*: "**PHONE.BAK ... JOHN.TXT**"
  Each file in the specified directory is listed, with its filename, extension, size in bytes, and the date/time it was last modified (the three files with the **BAK** extension are the automatically created *backup* versions of the text files you edited with **EDLIN**).

- The *status line*: "**9 File(s) 339968 bytes free**"
  DOS also shows how many files are currently in this directory and how many free bytes are still available on the disk.

As you can see, **DIR** tells you *a lot* in just this one screen. But...

What if: You list a **DIR**ectory with too many files to fit on one screen; the files scroll by too quickly to read. What do you do?

Aha: For many commands, DOS offers certain options, called switches, which you can specify For example, there's a *pause* switch for the **DIR** command. Instead of **DIR**, just enter **DIR /P**.... **The** listing pauses, a screenful at a time.

In fact, **DIR** has several such switches: **DIR /W** lists files side by side instead of top to bottom, omitting file sizes and date stamps. And there are other switches too.

The **Dir** command has two problems which can be very frustrating:

1. Some hidden files are not displayed, so you don't really know if you're seeing the whole picture.

2. The files are displayed in whatever random order they happen to be on the disk. If you're looking for a particular file, you must search the entire list.

Happily, MS-DOS 5.0 solves both of these problems:*

In the Dark: Put the *Boot* disk into the **A:** drive and type **DIR A:** [←ENTER].

The hidden system files are there, but you can't tell. How do you see them?

Turn on the Light: Type **DIR A: /A** [←ENTER].

Now, all of the files are displayed, even the hidden ones. The **/A** switch tells DOS to show "All" of the files.

---

*If you don't have DOS 5.0, you just have to live with these shortcomings. Skip these exercises and go ahead to page 142.

DOS 5 solves the second problem with the **/O** ("Order") switch....

What a Mess: Put the *Power* disk back into the **A:** drive and type **DIR A:** ◄—ENTER .

This is the jumbled mess you saw three pages ago. How can you put the files in alphabetical order?

Give the Order: Type **DIR A: /O** ◄—ENTER .

The files are displayed again, but this time in alphabetical order.

The best way to use these **DIR** switches is like ordering a pizza....

Try a Combo: Type **DIR A: /A /O /P** ◄—ENTER .

This will display "All" the files in "Order" and "Pause" between screens.

Too much typing? After you learn more about DOS, you can take a shortcut. It's explained on page 276.

The **/O** switch does more than just put files in order. It also lists the directories, if any, before the files. In order to appreciate this, you need to know more about directories....

Growing a Directory Tree

To grow a directory tree, you need to learn three important "gardener's tools:"

MD or **MKDIR** = Make Directory

CD or **CHDIR** = Change Directory

RD or **RMDIR** = Remove Directory*

With these three commands you can grow, climb through, and tear down directory trees. These are built-in commands--you do not have to worry about finding them on a disk.

Do This: Create a directory that grows out of (is a *sub-directory* of) the root directory on your *Power* disk.

Here's How: With the *Power* disk in drive **A :** , type:

MD FIRST [←ENTER]

That's it—you now have a new directory—a sub-directory of the root directory**—called **FIRST**.

Want To See? Just ask for a **DIR** listing: **DIR FIRST ....   Sure** enough—an empty directory, named as you requested!

---

*Some prefer to think of it as "Remove Deadwood."

**Since all directories you create grow out of the root directory—or out of others that you've created—they're all sub-directories of the root directory. Don't let the language confuse you: A subdirectory is simply another name for a directory that grows out of some other directory.

So, are you now working in your new **FIRST** directory? In other words, is it the *current* or *default* directory?

To find out, run a **DIR** without specifying which directory. This will tell you which directory is the *current* or *default* directory.... No—you're *not* in the **FIRST** directory yet—you're still in the root directory!

So Move: Change to your new directory.

Like So: Type **CD FIRST** ←ENTER.... Now run an unspecified **DIR** to prove it.... Now change back to the root directory once again: Type **CD ** ←ENTER.

Remember, you're changing directories (**CD**)—*you aren't changing disks.* You're just moving between different directories on the *same* disk.

Now Prune: Remove (throw away) your empty **FIRST** directory.

Like This: *Type:* **RD \FIRST** ←ENTER. That's it—gone (run a **DIR** now, if you want to check).

Keep in mind that you can remove a directory only if it's empty; if you had put any files or grown another directory in your **FIRST** directory, DOS would have refused to remove **FIRST** until all its contents were removed.

Tree Structures

Each disk has only one tree—starting at the root and branching out....

Grow: With your computer booted with the *Boot* disk and with the *Power* disk in disk drive **A:**, enter* the following commands to seed your tree:**

```
MD SOD
MD 123
MD DBASE
MD WORD
MD BATCH
MD EDITLINE
```

You can create directories with any names you choose—up to eight characters long. A word to the wise: Use meaningful words or abbreviations for everything (after awhile, simple acronyms or nondescript names start to look like alphabet soup when you try to remember what's what)!

Now you have a root directory with six subdirectories: **SOD**, **WORD**, **123**, **BATCH**, **DBASE**, and **EDITLINE**—and you can verify this with **DIR** (do it).... Notice the **DIR** extension listed for these directories—an easy way to see what's a file and what's a directory, no?

---

*Reminder: "enter" means "remember to press ⏎ENTER at the end of each command."

**Do not add fertilizer.

One of these directories, **WORD**, can contain your word processor and all documents made with that word processor.

Hmm...:   You write many different *kinds* of things with a word processor. How do you organize all these different documents?

Ah: Just grow additional directories *within* your **WORD** directory, by entering these commands:

CD WORD   This changes DOS's "attention" to **WORD**— it's now the *current* directory.

MD CLASSES   This makes a new directory, **CLASSES**, within **WORD**. A student might keep homework here.

MD PEOPLE There's another new directory, **PEOPLE**, within **WORD**—maybe for addresses and correspondence.

If a directory contains one or more subdirectories, it's called a *parent directory*. So, on your *Power* disk, the root directory is now the parent directory of **SOD**, **WORD**, **123**, **BATCH**, **DBASE**, and **EDITLINE**. And **WORD**, in turn, is the parent directory of **CLASSES** and **PEOPLE**.

To save you some typing, DOS lets you designate the current directory with a period (**.**); and the parent directory of the current directory with two periods (**..**).

For example: You've left your computer working in the **WORD** directory. To move back to its parent—the root directory—you could of course, enter **CD **. *Or*, you could enter **CD ..**   (do that now)..

Back to tree-growing: When you added directories **CLASSES** and **PEOPLE**, you first *changed* to the **WORD** directory—so that the new additions would be growing out of **WORD**. But did you *have* to change?

Question: *While staying in the root directory,* can you add three new offspring directories (**FRENCH**, **HISTORY**, and **PHYSICS**) to the *CLASSES* directory?

Yep: Enter these: **MD WORD\CLASSES\COMPUTER**
MD WORD\CLASSES\HISTORY
MD WORD\CLASSES\PHYSICS

As usual, if you want your command to affect somewhere else besides the current directory (that is, the current *path*), you simply specify the other path explicitly.

The **CLASSES** directory is now subdivided into **COMPUTER**, **HISTORY**, and **PHYSICS**. If you were a student doing your homework on the word processor, you could keep the different assignments separated by classes. Then, for example, if you want to work on your physics paper, you could go right to the **PHYSICS** directory to find it—easy!

Actually, though, the above solution required a lot of typing. It *would* have made your job easier simply to change to the **CLASSES** directory and create its offspring right there:

MD COMPUTER　　　　**MD HISTORY**　　　　**MD PHYSICS**

But—as with many aspects of DOS—the choice of methods is yours!

Changing Directory Names

Real trees need sod in which to grow—but that's not why you grew the **SOD** directory a few pages ago. **SOD** is just **DOS** spelled backwards—just to remind you that a directory named DOS is nothing official or sacred. But it _is_ rather convenient....

Switcheroo: Switch the **SOD** directory into the **DOS** directory.

The Change: From the root directory (you should already be there), enter the following: **RD SOD**
MD DOS

The empty **SOD** directory is now removed and an empty directory named **DOS** has been made.

Of course, you couldn't do the renaming this way (i.e. removing and re-making) if there were anything—files or subdirectories—already in **SOD**.

Moving Around Your Tree

You first learned about *pathnames* in Chapter 3. The pathname—as you now know—is the list of the parent and offspring directories you traverse through to arrive at a certain place in the tree. It's a map that directs DOS to a certain directory.

Path-ology: For each of the following **DIR** commands, what's the pathname and what directory will be displayed?

> a. **DIR **
> b. **DIR \WORD**
> c. **DIR \WORD\CLASSES\PHYSICS**

Solutions: a. The pathname is ****.
The root directory will be displayed.

b. The pathname is **\WORD**.
The **WORD** directory will be displayed.

c. The pathname is **\WORD\CLASSES\PHYSICS**.
The **PHYSICS** directory will be displayed.

Where Are You?

As you know, you use the **CD** (Change Directory) command to climb about the branches of your disk tree.

Question: Is there some way more convenient than constantly entering **DIR** to keep track of where you are?

Answer: Fortunately, yes. You can *change the DOS prompt* to tell you (remember how you learned to customize that prompt a little—pages 112-115)?

Enter this: **PROMPT PG** ....See? The prompt now shows you the full path of your current directory—no matter where you move. The **$P** tells DOS to show the path; the **$G** requests the **>**.

The perfect solution—right?

Well... not for everybody. It forces DOS to read the disk *every time* it displays the prompt, and that can cause problems. For example, if your current directory is supposed to be in the **A:** drive—but there's no disk there at the moment—DOS can't even give you a prompt, so it gives you an error message and wastes your time instead.

So for now, change your DOS prompt back to "plain," by entering **PROMPT**.

Next Move: Change to the **PEOPLE** directory (**CD PEOPLE**) and verify that you're actually there.

Here's How: First, enter **CD \WORD\PEOPLE** to move to that directory. Then, enter **CD** (nothing else) and DOS will show you that you've actually arrived—**CD** by itself shows you the current directory.

So you have a choice: You can keep the plain DOS prompt and use **CD** by itself occasionally to double-check your location. Or you can use **PROMPT PG** so that the prompt will always remind you.

OK, Tarzan: Try some tree-maneuvering practice. Enter these:

**CD **	To move to the root directory.
CD \123	To move to the **123** directory.
CD	To verify that.
CD \WORD	To move to the **WORD** directory.
CD PEOPLE	To move to the **PEOPLE** directory.
CD ..	To go to **PEOPLE**'s parent—**WORD**.
CD	To verify that.
**CD **	To "drop down" to the root directory.

Using Shortcuts and Defaults

In a directory tree of any size or complexity, you'll soon be using rather long pathnames, and the typing gets tedious. So shortcuts are helpful.

Suppose: You want to see **DIR**ectory listings of the **CLASSES** and **PEOPLE** directories. So enter **DIR \WORD\CLASSES** and there's the **CLASSES** listing.

But Now: Instead of typing everything from the start for the **PEOPLE** directory, just press F3 instead—to *repeat the last command.* Now you can edit this: Press DEL enough to erase **CLASSES**, then type **PEOPLE** in its place and press ←ENTER.... Voilá!

Other shortcuts involve your brain instead of a special function key. They involve taking advantage of the defaults to the fullest extent.

To prepare for an example of this, enter **CD \WORD\CLASSES**. This puts you somewhere in the middle of the tree (in the **CLASSES** directory, obviously—enter **CD** now to check this, if you wish).

You now have branches "below" you and "above" you. But you can view *any* directory from here. It just takes a little thought....

Hm: You now want to see directory listings of the current directory (**CLASSES**), its parent, the root, **DBASE**, and **COMPUTER** directories. Do this with full pathnames and then with shortcuts that use the defaults you now know.

OK: The default disk drive is **A:**, and the *default* (i.e. the current directory's) *pathname* is **\WORD\CLASSES**. So you can use the shortened pathnames in the list of **DIR** commands below; each is the equivalent of the full pathname:

Directory	Full Pathname	Short Pathname
CLASSES	DIR A:\WORD\CLASSES	DIR
Root	DIR A:\	DIR \
Parent	DIR A:\WORD	DIR ..
DBASE	DIR A:\DBASE	DIR \DBASE
COMPUTER	DIR A:\WORD\CLASSES\COMPUTER	DIR COMPUTER

Here's the rule: If you start a short pathname with a *backslash*, it means to start at the *root* and go upwards; otherwise, DOS will start at the current directory and go upwards. So, if you were to enter **DIR WORD** in the above situation, you'd get an error, because DOS would then try to find the directory called **A:\WORD\CLASSES\WORD**—and there's no such thing.

Now enter **CD ** to return to the root.

Shortened path names save a lot of typing, no? And remember that you can always use the [F3] key, too—to quickly rebuild similar commands.

Viewing Your Tree

You've learned how to view a listing of the files in a directory—with the **DIR** command—but how do you view a whole tree? If you use **DIR **, you'll see a list of the files in the root directory and also the **DOS**, **WORD**, **123**, **DBASE**, **BATCH**, and **EDITLINE** directories—but not the other directories. Not all branches of a tree grow off the trunk; neither do all of the directories of a disk tree grow off its root.

Of course, you could use the **DIR** command to show the directories which are not "attached" to the root by listing the directory for each of the subdirectories. But DOS does give you a way to view the entire tree at once—the **TREE** command (available on PC-DOS versions 2.00 and later and MS-DOS versions 3.2 and later; if you have an earlier version, then read—but don't do—the next example).

TREE is an external command, so it's more convenient to copy it into the DOS directory on your *Power* disk....

Do It: If you have a fixed disk, put the *Power* disk into the **A:** drive and enter: **COPY C:\DOS\TREE.* A:\DOS**

If you have only removable disks: Find which DOS working disk contains **TREE**: Put each DOS disk into the **A:** drive and use **DIR** until you find a file named **TREE.EXE** or **TREE.COM**. That's the disk. Then, if you have a **B:** drive, put the *Power* disk there; if not, DOS will tell you when to switch disks (to the *Power* disk). Then enter: **COPY A:TREE.* B:\DOS**

OK, you're ready to see the whole tree. ...

Try It: With the *Power* disk in the **A :** drive, enter **TREE**.

Result: You'll get this upside-down disk tree:*

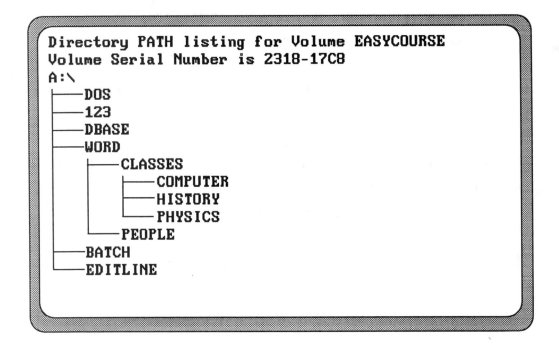

```
Directory PATH listing for Volume EASYCOURSE
Volume Serial Number is 2318-17C8
A:\
 ├──DOS
 ├──123
 ├──DBASE
 ├──WORD
 │    ├──CLASSES
 │    │    ├──COMPUTER
 │    │    ├──HISTORY
 │    │    └──PHYSICS
 │    └──PEOPLE
 ├──BATCH
 └──EDITLINE
```

*Some versions of DOS display this differently.

Another interesting way of looking at a disk tree is with the **CHKDSK** command. **CHKDSK** performs two functions:

- It repairs certain types of damaged disks;

- It displays a detailed record of a disk's contents.

Like **TREE**, **CHKDSK** is an external command and ought to be copied to the *Power* disk. This procedure should be getting familiar:

Ho Hum: If you have a fixed disk, with the *Power* disk in the A: drive, enter: **COPY C:\DOS\CHKDSK.* A:\DOS**

        If you have only removable disks, then use **DIR** to find which DOS working disk has a file named **CHKDSK.EXE** or **CHKDSK.COM**. Leave that disk in the drive and put the *Power* disk into **B:** (or wait for DOS's cue to put it into **A:**). Then enter: **COPY A:CHKDSK.* B:\DOS**

Then: Enter **CHKDSK**.... You'll see a bunch of numbers—not too exciting, right? But now use a *switch*—an option for the **CHKDSK** command: Enter **CHKDSK /V** (**V** for "*Verbose*")....

      Now *that's* a listing, eh? **CHKDSK** beats **DIR** and **TREE** all hollow when you want to see the big picture!

Unfortunately, part of your view scrolls off the screen. You'll soon see how to correct this (page 182).

Viewing Your Tree   **155**

What's in a Name?

Without directories, every filename on any one disk would have to be unique. For example, almost every new applications program you buy nowadays has a file named **README**—full of last-minute notes or instructions about the program. Without directories, only one **README** file could exist on a disk; every new program would overwrite the **README** file of the previous program!

But fortunately, you can put programs into separate directories—so each file named **README** can be stored in its own private space—all the **README**'s can co-exist.

Even directory names can be the same as filenames. Consider:

- **C:\WORD\DAVE**   (a file)
- **C:\123\DAVE**   (a file)
- **C:\DBASE\DAVE**   (a directory)

Hmm: If, as shown above, you had two files and a directory on the same disk—all with the same name (**DAVE**)—how would DOS tell them apart?

Easy: Notice that all the **DAVE**'s in this example are in three different directories (**WORD, 123**, and **DBASE**). The key is, *DAVE appears just once in any particular directory.* So if a command needs just a pathname, enter just the pathname. If it needs a filename, enter the filename. DOS will know the difference!

Changing Names

Of course, if a filename confuses you, you can always change it. The **RENAME** command (also called **REN**) does just that.

As you may recall, in the last chapter, on pages 128-132, you made a **MEMO.TXT** file, then edited it, and then finally erased it. And now the only evidence of this file on your *Power* disk is that file called **MEMO.BAK**—a BAcKup file made by **EDLIN**.

Danger: **MEMO.BAK** is in danger, because if you don't rename it, **EDLIN** would write over it the next time you wrote a **MEMO**. If you want to make this backup copy an original again, you have to change it back to a text file, right? What do you do?

This: You have two choices. With the *Power* disk in the **A:** drive, enter: **RENAME MEMO.BAK MEMO.TXT**
or: **REN MEMO.BAK MEMO.TXT**

Notice that since **REN** is an internal command, you didn't have to worry whether DOS would be able to find it.

So, are you getting a green thumb, with all this practice with directory trees?   Time to find out....

Stumpers

1. How is the directory command like a TV camera?

2. How do you keep a **DIR** display from scrolling by too fast to read?

3. Name the three vital directory commands.

4. How do you change the default directory to that of a disk in another disk drive?

5. Name the parts of a directory tree.

6. *Gardener's Challenge*:

   a. Climb the *Power Disk* tree to the **\WORD\PEOPLE** directory. Grow two more directories from this branch and name them **JOHN** and **TODD**.

   b. Return to the root directory tree in one step. From there, add a **MARY** directory to the **\WORD\PEOPLE** branch.

   c. From the root directory, remove the **TODD** directory.

7. How can you display the **PEOPLE** directory, from the root, to verify that the **JOHN** and **MARY** directories are actually there?

8. Enter **CD \WORD\CLASSES\HISTORY**. How can you prove that you're actually in the **HISTORY** directory?

9. You're balanced on the **PEOPLE** branch of the *Power* disk (i.e. you have entered **CD \WORD\PEOPLE** to get there). Now you want to see listings of the root, parent, **PEOPLE, DBASE,** and **MARY** directories. Show how to do this with full pathnames and with shortcuts that take advantage of the defaults.

10. Name three ways to view a tree.

11. Can more than one file on a disk have the same name?

12. When can a file and a directory have the same name? When can two directories have the same name?

13. Stop and think for a moment about the current situation on your *Power* disk: You've got several files in the root directory, plus a tree structure. What's wrong?

Wooden You Know It?

1. The **DIR** command sends a "picture" of a disk to the monitor so that you can see what's on the disk.

2. You can remedy this in two ways:

    -   Use the **Pause** switch: **DIR /P** displays just one screenful of the directory listing at a time.

    -   Use the **Wide** switch: **DIR /W** displays the files side-by-side so that they usually all fit on the screen at once.

3. The vital "3D's" of DOS trees are: **MD**   (Make Directory)
                                                        CD   (Change Directory)
                                                        RD   (Remove Directory)

4. To change the default directory to that of a disk on another drive:

    -   Change the default drive (for example, enter **A:** or **C:**).

    -   Then move to the desired directory of that drive, with the **CD** command.

5. The three parts of disk trees are

  - Root   The main directory;

  - Branches   The directories and subdirectories that "grow" up from the root;

  - Leaves   The programs and other files stored among the various branches.

6. With the *Power* disk in the **A:** drive:

   a. Enter: **CD \WORD\PEOPLE**
                      MD JOHN
                      MD TODD

   b. Enter: **CD **
                      MD \WORD\PEOPLE\MARY

   c. Enter: **RD \WORD\PEOPLE\TODD**

   The **JOHN** and **MARY** directories will remain (use these types of directories for letters to friends and relatives, client lists—whatever).

7. Enter **DIR \WORD\PEOPLE**

8. Enter **CD**

9. Remember that the default disk drive is **A:**, and the default pathname is **\WORD\PEOPLE**. Thus ...

Directory	Long Pathname	Short Pathname
PEOPLE	**DIR A:\WORD\PEOPLE**	**DIR**
Root	**DIR A:**	**DIR **
Parent	**DIR A:\WORD**	**DIR ..**
DBASE	**DIR A:\DBASE**	**DIR \DBASE**
MARY	**DIR A:\WORD\PEOPLE\MARY**	**DIR MARY**

(Enter **CD ** to return to the root.)

10. The three ways to view a disk tree are:

DIR — This won't show you the entire tree at once, however—only the branches (and files) in a particular directory.

TREE — This is probably best for quick checks—a concise diagram of the disk tree. Also, try **TREE /F** to see the files, too

CHKDSK /V — The verbose switch (**/V**) gives you a detailed listing of your tree structure.

11. Files in *different directories* can have the same name.

12. A file and a directory can have the same name—as long as they aren't both in the same directory. Directories can also share a common name—again, as long as they don't both grow from the same directory.

13. The files aren't distributed into their appropriate directories. After all, the purpose of the directories is to *organize* the files into similar categories. So long as you keep dumping most of your files together in the root directory, you're not accomplishing this goal.

The next chapter will show you how to put your files where they belong ...

9. MOVING YOUR FILES AROUND

Copying Files

Imagine sitting at a rolltop desk. You take a file out of a cubbyhole, copy it and put the original back where you got it. Then you put the new copy into another cubbyhole.

This is how DOS moves files around for you—by *copying*. If you load a file from a disk into the computer's memory, the file is still on the disk; if you then print it, the file is on the disk, in memory, and also sent to the printer!

This chapter demonstrates how to use all sorts of useful commands to move files around and process them in various ways. Many people learn the bare **COPY** command and think that's all there is to it. That's like using a Harley-Davidson as a scooter. **COPY** is a sophisticated command that can do a lot of hard work for you—and then there are **XCOPY** and **DISKCOPY**.

But, first, start copying files with a simple command you've seen already....

The TYPE Command

Remember when you used the **TYPE** command to make text files on disk and display them on the monitor? Well, generally speaking, **TYPE** moves a copy of any given file from one place to another (leaving the original file at the first location).

Example: How would you use **TYPE** to copy the **MEMO.TXT** file on the *Power* disk from the root directory to the **\EDITLINE** directory?*

Solution: Enter this (all on one line):

TYPE MEMO.TXT > \EDITLINE\MEMO.TXT

What's happening here? To examine this lengthy command sentence just break it down into its logical parts:

TYPE	the command itself
MEMO.TXT	the file to be moved (the *source* file)
>	the "to" symbol, which means "send the file here"
\EDITLINE	the pathname of that destination
MEMO.TXT	the name of the destination file

---

*All the examples in this chapter assume that you have booted your computer with your *Boot* disk, that **A:** is the default disk drive, and, unless otherwise specified, the *Power* disk is in that **A:** drive.

The COPY Command

Though **TYPE** can do the job—as you've seen—the **COPY** command was custom-made for copying files. It, too, copies a file from one location to another, leaving the original file as it was.

The brief syntax of the **COPY** command is:

COPY _Source Destination_

Source   The **source parameter** is the full pathname of the file to be copied—including the drive, directory(s) and filename. If you don't specify a pathname, DOS uses the default path.

Destination   The **destination parameter** is the pathname where the copy file is to be sent. This means you can change the name of the copy—send it to a file with a name different than the original.

Try It: Display the contents of the text file **JOHN.TXT**.

Do This: Enter **COPY JOHN.TXT CON**

The contents of the source file (**JOHN.TXT**) are copied to the destination—the **CON**sole (monitor).

Remember when you used **TYPE** to send your keystrokes directly from the keyboard (the **CON**sole) into a file (pages 124-126)? Well, you can do this with **COPY**, too:

Challenge: Create a new text file, called **COPY.TXT**, onto your *Power* disk—in the **COMPUTER** directory—containing this text: **I am copying from the CONsole to the COPY.TXT file on the disk!**

Solution: Enter this command:
COPY CON \WORD\CLASSES\COMPUTER\COPY.TXT

Now *type:* **I am copying from the CONsole to the COPY.TXT file on the disk!**

Now press F6—the caboose byte (EOF)—and ←ENTER to end the file. You now have the **COPY.TXT** file on your *Power* disk.

Notice: The **COPY.TXT** has nothing whatsoever to do with the **COPY** command. That all-important **TXT** extension tells you it's a text file—not a command.

You might wonder why both the **TYPE** and **COPY** commands do so many of the same things—why not just have one command to do them?

Answer: Personal preference! Microsoft realized that different people like to do things different ways (and if you can't remember how to do something one way, maybe you'll remember it the other way).

Besides, there *are* differences between **COPY** and **TYPE**: The real strength of **COPY** lies in moving files ...

So: With what you know about **COPY**, can you move **JOHN.TXT** from the root to the **\WORD\PEOPLE\JOHN** directory?

Sure: Enter this: **COPY JOHN.TXT \WORD\PEOPLE\JOHN**

Caution: DOS will wipe out any file with the same name in your destination directory. For example, if a file named **JOHN.TXT** already exists in the **JOHN** directory, DOS would replace it with the **JOHN.TXT** file being copied from the root directory.

More: **COPY** these remaining seven files from the root directory to the **EDITLINE** directory.

SHOP.BAK	PHONE.TXT	
SHOP.TXT	PHONE.BAK	ADDRESS.TXT
TODO.TXT	EDLIN.COM	

Do It: Enter: COPY SHOP.BAK EDITLINE
COPY SHOP.TXT EDITLINE
COPY TODO.TXT EDITLINE
COPY PHONE.BAK EDITLINE
COPY EDLIN.COM EDITLINE
COPY PHONE.TXT EDITLINE
COPY ADDRESS.TXT EDITLINE

Wildcards

That previous example took a lot of typing (sorry about that). As usual there's an easier way: **Wildcards.** Wildcards are *placeholders* that you can use to represent parts of filenames to save you typing.

Example: Suppose you decide that your text (**.TXT**) files should all be kept in the **WORD** directory rather than in **EDITLINE**. Use one **COPY** command to do this.

Solution: Enter: **COPY \EDITLINE*.TXT \WORD**

The source parameter is **\EDITLINE*.TXT**. The filename ***.TXT** specifies *all files* (in the specified directory) *with a .TXT extension*. The ***** means "whatever," and so all the **.TXT** files in **EDITLINE** are copied to **WORD**. But the files **PHONE.BAK, EDLIN.COM**, and **SHOP.BAK** are *not* copied, because they don't meet the **.TXT** specification—they have different extensions.

Try This: Use a single **COPY** command to copy **PHONE.TXT** and **PHONE.BAK** from **EDITLINE** to **DBASE**.

Solution: Enter: **COPY \EDITLINE\PHONE.* \DBASE**

The source parameter is **\EDITLINE\PHONE.***. The **PHONE.*** specifies *all files* (in the specified directory) *named PHONE*—no matter what the extensions are. So both **PHONE.TXT** and **PHONE.BAK** are copied.

Now: Suppose you want to cleanup the root directory. All files in the root have been copied to other directories, so now you want to **ERASE** these originals—all in one command.

Easy: Enter: **ERASE *.***

That's a very short but powerful command! The ***.*** means *every file* (in the specified directory)—no matter what its name or extension. Here the "specified" directory was simply the root directory (because it's the default).

Notice that DOS asks you to verify that you want to go through with this **ERASE** process—and for good reason: Mistaken use of ***.*** can instantly destroy a lot of valuable files!

One More: With a single **COPY** command, copy all files in the **\WORD** directory to the **\WORD\PEOPLE** directory. Then erase the original files with just one more command.

Solution: Enter these: **COPY \WORD*.* \WORD\PEOPLE**
ERASE \WORD*.*

The first command copies all (***.***) files from the **\WORD** directory to the **\WORD\PEOPLE** directory. The second command erases the originals.

So that's the basic idea of *****. Use it with caution—but use it—whenever you can to save yourself repetitive commands and typing.

There's another useful wildcard—the **?** wildcard—that requires a little more finesse....

Try This: The one file in the **JOHN** directory is **JOHN.TXT**. But what if you want to put more text files about John in this directory? You can't name them all **JOHN.TXT**. Hmm.... How about naming the first file **JOHN0001.TXT**, the second one **JOHN0002.TXT**, etc.?

Do This: Enter **CD \WORD\PEOPLE\JOHN** (to change to the **JOHN** directory). Then enter:

```
RENAME JOHN.TXT JOHN0001.TXT
COPY JOHN0001.TXT JOHN0002.TXT
COPY JOHN0002.TXT JOHN9999.TXT
```

Instead of one file named **JOHN.TXT**, you now have:

```
JOHN0001.TXT    JOHN0002.TXT
                JOHN9999.TXT.
```

Now, try the **?** wildcard, by entering this:

```
COPY JOHN????.TXT \123
```

All these new **JOHN** files are copied to the **123** directory!

That's how the **?** wildcard works—it substitutes for any single *character* in a pathname.

Now enter **CD ** to return to the root directory.

The XCOPY Command

What if you want to copy everything in a directory—including any subdirectories? DOS provides **XCOPY** (eXtended **COPY**) for this.

XCOPY is an external command in versions 3.2 and greater, so in order to use it conveniently, first you ought to place it on your *Power* disk.

Do It: If you have a fixed disk, put the *Power* disk into the A: drive, and enter: `COPY C:\DOS\XCOPY.* A:\DOS`

If you have just removable disks, find which DOS working disk contains a file named `XCOPY.COM` or `XCOPY.EXE`. Leave that disk in the drive. Put the *Power* disk into the **B:** drive, if any, or wait for DOS to tell you to put it into the **A:** drive.

Enter `COPY A:XCOPY.* B:\DOS`

Question: Why the * wildcard?

Answer: Your **XCOPY** command file may have either a `.COM` or `.EXE` extension. By entering `XCOPY.*` you allow for both possibilities—so you don't have to bother remembering which extension you have.

Now it's ready for action, so practice with **XCOPY**....

Problem: Copy the entire **PEOPLE** directory—even the **JOHN** and **MARY** subdirectories and their files—to the **EDITLINE** directory.

Solution: Enter this:

XCOPY \WORD\PEOPLE*.* \EDITLINE /S /E

\WORD\PEOPLE*.* is the *source* parameter—the stuff to be copied. **\EDITLINE** is the *destination*.

/S is a switch telling DOS to copy even the subdirectories. **/E** is a switch telling DOS to copy even the *empty* ones.

Uh...:   What has this done to the disk? What does it mean to "copy subdirectories?" What does the disk look like now?

Look: Enter **TREE**. See? The **MARY** and **JOHN** subdirectories are now in two places: **PEOPLE** and **EDITLINE**.

XCOPY is a rather powerful command, isn't it? Besides moving files, it can also move subdirectories (and their subdirectories and files, etc.).

The DISKCOPY Command

What if you want to copy an entire *disk* to another disk? The **DISKCOPY** command is made for this. You've already seen it in action back in Chapter 4, but now you can look at it with a little more understanding:

Review: Copy the entire *Power* disk to the *Power Backup* disk.

Like So: If you have a fixed disk, enter **DISKCOPY A: A:** and follow the directions on the screen. If you have only removable disks, find the DOS working disk containing the **DISKCOPY** file. With that disk in the **A:** drive, enter **DISKCOPY A: A:** and follow the directions on the video.

So you have many ways to copy files: **TYPE**, **COPY**, **XCOPY**, and **DISKCOPY**, to name a few.

The SYS Command

Remember the **IO.SYS** and **MSDOS.SYS** files—loaded into memory at boot time? For protection, these *system* files require special handling (you can't use **TYPE** or **COPY**, but you can use **DISKCOPY***).

Do This: Put your *Boot* disk in the **A:** drive and enter **DIR**. You don't see **IO.SYS** or **MSDOS.SYS** listed, do you? They *are* there, but they don't show in the directory listing.

But: DOS has a special (external) command to copy just these two files. Try it: copy the system files onto the *Boot Backup* disk: With a fixed disk, put the *Boot Backup* disk into the **A:** drive, and **C:** [←ENTER], **SYS A:** [←ENTER], **A:** [←ENTER].

Or—if you have only removable disks—locate the DOS working disk with the **SYS** command file and place this disk into the **A:** drive. If you have a **B:** drive, put the *Boot Backup* disk there; otherwise, put it into the **A:** drive when instructed to by the video screen. Enter **SYS B:**

That's it—you've copied the two system files, **IO.SYS** and **MSDOS.SYS**. Can the *Boot Disk Backup* now boot the computer? No, it doesn't have the **COMMAND.COM** file—the command interpreter (shell) program.** You can copy **COMMAND.COM** with the **COPY** command.

*Remember, too, that when you **FORMAT** your boot disks with the **/S** switch, that automatically copies the system files to the newly formatted disks.

Unless you're running DOS 5, which *does* copy **COMMAND.COM with the **SYS** command.

Verifying Your Copies

Do you sometimes wonder if a file was really copied correctly? DOS offers you ways to reassure yourself.

Of course, you have the **DIR** command, but there are some others you ought to know about now:

- **COMP** (**COMP**are), is an external command in all PC-DOS versions and in MS-DOS since version 3.3.

- **FC**, for **F**ile **C**ompare, is an external command in MS-DOS versions 2.00 and greater.

- **DISKCOMP**, (**DISK COMP**are), is external. It's in all _PC-DOS_ versions and in _MS-DOS_ since version 3.2.

Since all of these three commands are external, they must be on a disk which is accessible to DOS. If you have a fixed disk, this is already the case. If you don't, then (guess what?) you must copy the files to the _Power Disk_ first.

You've already had plenty of experience doing this with other external commands, so this time, do it yourself (remember that you can use the * wildcard for the filename extensions (**COMP.***, **FC.***, and **DISKCOMP.***)....

When you've done it, turn the page....

Juxtapose: Place the *Power* disk into the A: drive and move to the **EDITLINE** directory (enter **CD \EDITLINE**). Now enter **DIR** and you'll see two files, named **PHONE.TXT** and **PHONE.BAK**. Are these two files the same?

Check #1: If your version of DOS has **COMP**, then enter

COMP PHONE.TXT PHONE.BAK

You'll get a message that the files are not the same size (so they can't be the same). Of course, you could have seen that by just looking at the file sizes in the directory listing, but ...

Check #2: If your version of DOS has **FC**, then enter **FC PHONE.TXT PHONE.BAK**. Instead of a rude message, you get a list of the differences between the two files. That's more courteous, isn't it?

Try Another: Compare the *Power* disk with the *Power Backup* disk.

Like This: With the *Power Disk* in the **A:** drive, enter

DISKCOMP A: A:

Then follow the directions on the screen.

The disks will not match. Put the *Power* disk into the **A:** drive and enter **CD **.

The VERIFY Command

The **COMP**, **FC**, and **DISKCOMP** commands may be helpful at one time or another, but they all require *after-the-fact* checking of your copied files' integrities. If you want to "check as you go," there's an easier way—the **VERIFY** command.

You turn VERIFY on, and it will do its job until you turn it off again: Every time a file is copied, the new copy is read back and compared with the original. And all this is done in the background—invisible to you on the monitor.

Questions: Is **VERIFY** on or off at the moment? How can you tell? How can you change it?

Simple: First, just enter **VERIFY**.

DOS will tell you that **VERIFY** is either **ON** or **OFF**. Then, to turn it on, enter **VERIFY ON**. Or, to turn it off, enter **VERIFY OFF**.

Is **VERIFY** a good idea? There is an advantage and a disadvantage:

VERIFY gives you the piece of mind that a file has been actually copied correctly (advantage). But with **VERIFY** on, the file-copying process takes longer (disadvantage).

So *you* decide.

Processing Files

All right, enough about copying. Just as important is how you can process files with DOS—*combine* them, *sort* them, *filter* them, and *route* them to different destinations.

Try This: Use the **COPY** command to somehow *append* the contents of **JOHN0002.TXT** to the end of **JOHN0001.TXT** (both are in the **123** directory on your *Power* disk).

Like So: Enter: **CD \123**
And: **COPY JOHN0001.TXT + JOHN0002.TXT**

Now **JOHN0001.TXT** file contains the contents of both original files; the second file was "added" to the first file. To see this, enter **TYPE JOHN0001.TXT**

Another: Use the **TYPE** command to append **JOHN0002.TXT** to the **JOHN0001.TXT** file, located in the **EDITLINE\JOHN** directory.

On target: Enter: **CD \EDITLINE\JOHN**
And: **TYPE JOHN0002.TXT >> JOHN0001.TXT**

As you've seen in other DOS commands, the **>** means "put it there and *overwrite* whatever's there now." But the **>>** means "put it there, *following* whatever's there now." Again, to see the results of this *appending*, enter **TYPE JOHN0001.TXT**.   Then enter **CD **.

Pipes and Filters

As you've seen with lots of commands—and now with those ❭ and ❭❭, DOS uses a lot of the _source-destination_ idea: "Get a file _from_ here and send it _to_ there." Well, what if you were to ask it to _do something to it in transit_—like filtering water as you pipe it around?...

Indeed, DOS has such a "plumbing" system: It uses pipes and filters to process files "in transit." A _pipe_ redirects a file through a _filter_, where a command is done on this file "in transit."

DOS has three such filters:

- **MORE**   This filter lets only a screenful of text through at a time.

- **SORT**   This filter lets a file through only in alphabetical order.

- **FIND**   This filter lets the lines of a file through that you specify.

All three filters are external commands in DOS versions 2.00 and greater, so if you don't have a fixed disk,* you should **COPY** the above three command files from the DOS working disks to the _Power_ disk (and to avoid worrying about differences in these files' extensions, use the filenames **MORE.***, **SORT.***, and **FIND.***).

Now, with the _Power_ disk in the **A:** drive, you're ready to do some simple computer file processing—some "plumbing."

*Perhaps by now you're considering getting a fixed disk to avoid this extra hassle?

Gusher: The *Power* disk is getting pretty crowded with files by now. Better check it out—enter **CHKDSK /V** and... oops—the display just spills off the top of the page. Can you slow this down to look at it—say, with a Pause switch?

Fixed: Not with a Pause switch (that's only for **DIR**.) But you can slow the output down by *piping* it through a *filter*:

Enter **CHKDSK /V ¦ MORE** ...See? The pipe character (¦ —the shifted \ key) tells DOS that the next command is a filter—in this case, **MORE**. Try these commands, too: **DIR \DOS ¦ MORE** and **TREE /F ¦ MORE**

Also: Unless you're using DOS 5 (see pages 140-141), any large directory listing can be frustrating when you're looking for a particular file. The **SORT** filter helps by sorting the files alphabetically.

Enter this: **DIR \DOS ¦ SORT** See what happens?

And you can **SORT** by filename, extension, or file size. Just specify which column of text to sort on. For example, in the **DIR** listing, the filename extensions begin in the tenth column. So, try this: **DIR \DOS ¦ SORT /+10**

The **/+10** switch tells DOS to sort on the tenth column.

Or, try this: **DIR \DOS ¦ SORT /+14**

This command sorts the files by size—smallest to largest—as you can see from the file sizes listed at column 14.

Obviously, these filters can be really useful, but there's one that's the slickest of them all—the **FIND** filter: **FIND** *selects only those items in a file that contain the character pattern you specify.*

Example: Do a directory listing that displays only directories —it filters out filenames (hint: look at a directory listing for a string of characters found only in directory items).

Solution: The string of characters **⟨DIR⟩** is unique to directory items in the listing. So enter **DIR ¦ FIND "⟨DIR⟩"** Voilá—only directories!

Now: Do a **DIR**ectory command that uses *all three* filters.

Like: **DIR ¦ FIND "⟨DIR⟩" ¦ SORT ¦ MORE**

What would you get? A **DIR**ectory listing showing only items containing **⟨DIR⟩**, sorted alphabetically and displayed one screenful at a time.

Also: Can a filter be used more than once?

Yep: **CHKDSK /V ¦ FIND "Directory" ¦ FIND "JOHN"**

is a good example: From a full **CHKDSK** listing; DOS extracts lines containing **Directory** *and* containing **JOHN**.

The result is a short list—the two **JOHN** directories!

Using Filters as Commands

Because filters are indeed commands, you can also use them as such—without a **DIR**, or **COPY**, or anything else in front. So keep in mind the *from* and *to* symbols (**<** and **>**) and how to use them:

< = "get it from here"   **>** = "put it there"

Try This: Alphabetize the telephone list in **PHONE.TXT**.

Fixup: Enter this command (all on one long line):
SORT < \EDITLINE\PHONE.TXT >
                              \EDITLINE\PHONE2.TXT
Now analyze each of this command's five parts:
SORT   (the command itself)
<   (get it *from* this source)
\EDITLINE\PHONE.TXT (the source)
>   (send it *to* this destination)
\EDITLINE\PHONE2.TXT   (the destination)
Enter **TYPE \EDITLINE\PHONE2.TXT** (the result)

Next: Do the same thing with **ADDRESS.TXT**.

OK: Try **SORT < \EDITLINE\ADDRESS.TXT**   (the output path isn't specified; it goes to the default—the CONsole)....

**460 S.W. Madison Ave., Suite 1
Corvallis, OR 97339
Grapevine Publications, Inc.
P.O. Box 2449**

Do you understand what happened there? **SORT** alphabetizes *line-by-line*, so it messes up multi-line entries, such as this address. That's no problem on this short sample file, but use filters cautiously on big files!

Example: Here's a bigger file: Run **CHKDSK** on a disk and then save the report in a file for future reference.

Like This: **CHKDSK /V > \DOS\DISK.TXT**

This says "send the **CHKDSK /V** listing to the **DISK.TXT** file in the **DOS** directory." So you don't *see* anything on the screen—the listing was sent to a disk file instead.

OK, But: What's the point of doing that unless you can *view* that file later? So how do you view the **DISK.TXT** file with the **CHKDSK** listing you just made?

Hmm...: If you enter **TYPE \DOS\DISK.TXT**, the listing will scroll by too fast to read (try it). How about using **MORE**?

You can use it as a filter for another command:
TYPE \DOS\DISK.TXT ¦ MORE

Or, you can use it as the command itself:
MORE < \DOS\DISK.TXT

Either way, you'll see the file a screenful at a time!

Printing Files

In all this processing and routing of files, don't forget your "paper route:" DOS offers you some nifty printing tricks.

Just as **CON** stands for **CON**sole, **PRN** stands for the **PR**i**N**ter. It's a reserved word to denote that particular *output device* (if you don't have a printer, you can skip these two pages; if you do have one, make sure it's on and ready, then continue here)....

Try These: **DIR > PRN**
                      TREE > PRN
                      CHKDSK /V > PRN

                      In these cases, a listing is *created* by the command and then sent to the printer instead of the monitor. But existing files can be sent to the printer, too

Like This: **COPY \EDITLINE\ADDRESS.TXT PRN**
                      TYPE \EDITLINE\TODO.TXT > PRN

Challenge: Send text directly from your keyboard to the printer.

Solution: **TYPE CON > PRN** [←ENTER], then **I am copying directly from the CONsole to the PRiNter!**

                      Press [F6][←ENTER] to end the command.... Voilá—your computer is now just a glorified typewriter!

PRN has some nifty capabilities, but the real industrial-strength printing command is **PRINT**—an external* command available in DOS versions 2.00 and greater.

Try It: Enter **PRINT \EDITLINE\MEMO.TXT**

(The first time you use **PRINT**, the display may ask you to enter the "list device." Just press (←ENTER) to select the printer. Then the file will print.)

This may not seem very powerful at first glance—indeed no different than **PRN**. But the beauty of **PRINT** is that it's the only DOS command that will let you do something else while it works. That is, the **PRINT** command works *in the background*.

So, for example, you can give **PRINT** commands for several files—in quick succession—then go on to other tasks on your computer. And all the while DOS will be printing the files—in the order you specified (just don't remove the disk containing the files being printed)!

*No fixed disk? **COPY** the **PRINT** command from its DOS working disk to the **DOS** directory on the *Power* disk.

Notes (Yours)

Filing in the Gaps

1. When a file is copied, what happens to the original?

2. What information does DOS need to execute a **COPY** command?

3. When you use **COPY** to *create* (not copy) a brand-new file on a disk, what's the source?

4. On the *Power* disk, copy **PHONE2.TXT** from the **EDITLINE** directory into the **WORD/PEOPLE** directory.

5. These files are in both the **EDITLINE** and **WORD/PEOPLE** directories: **ADDRESS.TXT, TODO.TXT, MEMO.TXT, PHONE.TXT, SHOP.TXT**, and **PHONE2.TXT**. Your mission: Erase them from the **EDITLINE** directory—with only one command.

6. What does a **?** mean to DOS?

7. What's the difference between **JOHN*.TXT** and **JOHN?.TXT**?

8. What's the primary difference between **COPY** and **XCOPY**?

9. What three commands compare files?

10. When would you ever enter **VERIFY ON**?

11. How are **>>** and **+** similar? Different?

12. What are pipes and filters?

13. Is the **EDLIN** command in the **DOS** directory of the *Power* disk? Is it in any of the directories on that disk?

14. What's the best way to print a list of every file on the *Power* disk?

15. Can DOS print a file while you do other work on the computer?

16. How would you use **DISKCOPY** to copy a fixed disk?

All Filed Out

1. When a file is copied, the original remains the same.

2. The syntax for the **COPY** command is **COPY** *Source Destination*. So the two pieces of information DOS needs are the

Source	The pathname of the file to be copied (and this may include wildcards).
Destination	The pathname where a copy of a file is to be placed.

3. The *source* is your **CON**sole (keyboard): **COPY CON** *Destination* where *Destination* is a filename.

4. Enter **COPY \EDITLINE\PHONE2.TXT \WORD\PEOPLE**

5. All those six files end with a **.TXT** extension, so you can enter **ERASE \EDITLINE*.TXT** to erase them all (do it now). Any other **.TXT** files in this directory will also be erased.

6. A **?** in DOS is a *wildcard* that tells DOS that any single character may be substituted in its position.

7. The ***** in **JOHN*.TXT** stands for one *or more* characters. Thus, **JOHN*.TXT** would include both **JOHN0001.TXT** and **JOHN1.TXT**.

The **?** in **JOHN?.TXT** stands for *only one* character. Thus, **JOHN?.TXT** wouldn't include **JOHN0001.TXT** but would include **JOHN1.TXT**.

8. The primary difference between **COPY** and **XCOPY** is that **COPY** will not copy subdirectories, but **XCOPY** will.

9. Three DOS commands compare files to see if they're the same: **COMP** and **FC** both compare two files at a time. **DISKCOMP** compares two entire disks.

10. Whenever you want to request that DOS verify every file it copies, you should enter **VERIFY ON**. To turn this feature off, enter **VERIFY OFF**. To find out whether it's currently on or off, just enter **VERIFY**.

11. Both operators, **>>** and **+**, combine two files into one (appending their contents). **+** is for **COPY**; **>>** is for other DOS commands:

```
COPY JOHN0001.TXT + JOHN0002.TXT
TYPE JOHN0002.TXT >> JOHN0001.TXT
```

Both examples attach (append) the **JOHN0002.TXT** file to the end of the **JOHN0001.TXT** file.

12. A pipe is the ¦ character, and it tells DOS that the next word in a command will be a filter—a command that alters a file "in transit." DOS has three such filters: **SORT**, **FIND**, and **MORE**.

13. To see if **EDLIN** is in the **DOS** directory, enter **DIR \DOS\EDLIN.***. You'll get a **File not found** message— **EDLIN** isn't there. Note that you're asking DOS here to list a particular *file*—perfectly acceptable with **DIR**. Either the file is there or it isn't.

   So just where is **EDLIN**? Use the **FIND** filter with a listing of the whole tree: **CHKDSK /V ¦ FIND "EDLIN"**

   You'll see: **A:\EDITLINE\EDLIN.COM**

   EDLIN is in the **EDITLINE** directory.

14. Enter **CHKDSK /V > PRN.**...   **The** (verbose) **CHKDSK** listing of every file on the disk will be printed.

15. Just enter **PRINT** *Filename* and DOS will print that file while you do other work on the computer (the disk with the file being printed must remain in the disk drive).

16. You can't—**DISKCOPY** won't work on fixed disks. For strategies about backing up files on fixed disks, read on ...

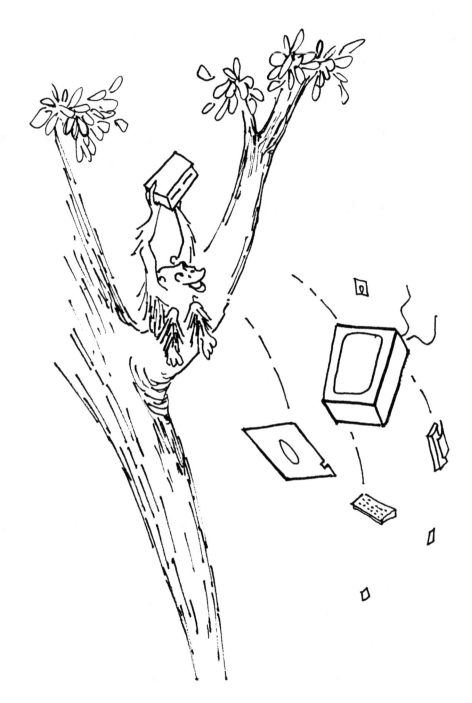

10. PROTECTING YOUR FILES

The Hazards

Murphy's Law has entered the computer age: *If anything can go wrong with your computer files, it will—at the worst possible moment.* And lots of things can go wrong. This chapter shows you how to protect yourself from these and other possible catastrophes:

Viruses

No loss of data is pleasant, but computer viruses are particularly nasty, because they are results of deliberate, malicious intents by real persons to do exactly that. A *computer* virus is a piece of program code designed to grow and/or duplicate—and wreak other havoc—in a computer's memory. Some also erase disks, leave obscene messages on the screen, etc. In short, a computer virus is a form of vandalism.

However, computer viruses were also used with honorable—if ill-advised—intentions, to protect application programs: If you *illegally copied* such a program for a friend, you risked activating the virus. This practice has all but stopped now, as the wider dangers of malicious viruses have become apparent.

To protect your computer from viruses of any kind:

- Don't copy programs illegally.

- Don't accept programs from persons of questionable judgement.

- Beware of programs downloaded from computer bulletin boards.

Be careful, but cool. Practice safe computing.

System Crashes

Has your computer crashed, yet? If it hasn't, it probably will sometime. Here are the typical types of crashes:

- The read/write head in your disk drive crashes into the rapidly-spinning magnetic surface of the disk, destroying some or all of the files—particularly painful on a *fixed disk* full of data.

- A program goes AWOL (Absent With Out Leave) from its allotted memory space and goes frolicking through the rest of RAM. Usually, the keyboard freezes, you have to reboot, and you lose whatever was in memory. But you can also lose disk files.

- You/friends/kids spill food/liquid into the keyboard/disk, resulting in loss of data/temper.

- You spend hours working on a project on the computer—but without periodically saving your file to a disk. Then, somehow* the power goes out.... Hours of work—gone.

Pilot Error

Yep—that's you. These are the easy mistakes to make if you're tired or distracted:

> You **overwrite** a valuable file—say, with **COPY**—mistakenly naming that file as the *destination.... Deep* doo-doo.

> You **ERASE** or **DEL** a valuable file.... Not so good, either.

*Maybe a real power outage, but more often, somebody stumbles over the cord, unplugging the computer. Or, how about this one? Somebody sets some books down in front of the computer, bumping the reset button, rebooting the computer, and losing your data.

Protecting Disks

With all these hazards—plus abuse by software pirates—it's no wonder that the software industry has devised ways to protect programs.

Copy Protection

If a program file doesn't copy or run correctly, its disk may have been **copy protected**—to prevent illegal copying—in one of these ways:

- The program's disk comes with a certain volume label. The program checks for the correct volume label before it will run.

- One or more sectors on the disk have a size other than 512 bytes. DOS won't copy it correctly, and so the program is copy-protected.

- The programmer hides an essential file on the disk. Most people, won't be aware of the hidden file. Thus, the new copy won't run!

And of course, there are ever-more-complex copy-protection schemes, as the software industry tries to stay ahead of the pirates.

Write Protection

Also, a floppy disk's files can be *physically* protected: Notice the little notch on the side of the disk*. If you cover the notch—with stickers usually provided—the disk's files *cannot be altered or erased*; they are **write-protected**. Expose the notch,** and the protection disappears.

*On a microdisk, there's a little plastic tab you slide forward.

** Or slide back the tab on the microdisk.

Protecting Files

What if you want to protect certain files—instead of a whole disk? This is the major topic for this chapter....

The **ATTRIB** Command

One way to do it is with the **ATTRIB** (ATTRIBute) command.* Each file has an *attribute byte*, located in that file's directory entry on the disk. The bits in this byte represent information about the file:

- *System* bit: If this bit is set, it means that the file is a *system file* (such as **IO.SYS** and **MSDOS.SYS**, as you read on pages 70-72).

- *Read-only* bit: If this bit is set, the file can be read from, but not written to or erased.

- *Hidden* bit: When this bit is set, DOS "hides" a file from some directory listings

- *Archive* bit: This bit is very useful when you're backing up files (you'll do this a little later in this chapter).

The **ATTRIB** command adjusts only the *Read-only* and *Archive* bits (apparently, Microsoft wanted you to have *some* access to these attribute bits—but not enough to hurt yourself).

*****ATTRIB** is an external command available in DOS versions 3.00 and greater. If you don't have a fixed disk, you should copy **ATTRIB** to the *Power* disk now (and you know the drill by now, right?).

To practice with the **ATTRIB** command, go to the **\WORD\PEOPLE** directory (ahem—enter **CD \WORD\PEOPLE**). Then:

Hmm: Is the Read-only or Archive bit set in the **PHONE.TXT** file?

Look: Enter **ATTRIB PHONE.TXT** and you'll see an **A**—the Archive bit is set. You *don't* see an **R**, so the Read-only bit is *not* set.

OK: Suppose you want to protect (only) this **PHONE.TXT** file from being changed. How do you do it?

Watch: Enter **ATTRIB +R PHONE.TXT**. The **+R** sets the Read-only bit. If you try to write to **PHONE.TXT** now, you'll get an error message.

Try It: Enter **COPY PHONE2.TXT PHONE.TXT** ....yep—an error —**PHONE.TXT** can't be changed! (Now enter **CD **).

So, if you have an important file which won't need changes very often, you can use **ATTRIB** to set its Read-only bit so that you won't accidentally erase or alter the file in the meantime.

In summary, the **ATTRIB** command has five variations:

ATTRIB +A *Filename*	sets the Archive bit.
ATTRIB -A *Filename*	clears the Archive bit.
ATTRIB +R *Filename*	sets the Read-only bit.
ATTRIB -R *Filename*	clears the Read-only bit.
ATTRIB *Filename*	shows the current states of these bits

And DOS 5 also has settings for the System and Hidden bits.

Password Protection

Another way to protect your files is through a password scheme—usually available through a shell, such as the DOS Shell. Briefly, here's how it works:

In the DOS Shell, you can create a menu system to start programs for you. As you do this, you can assign a password to each separate program. Then, when the program is chosen from the menu, it doesn't start until the correct password is entered. If you set up your shell to automatically start each time your computer is booted, then theoretically, nobody can get at your files except through the authorized passwords at your menu. But...

Stop and Think: If you wanted access to files on someone else's computer that was protected by a password scheme like the one above, how could you do it?

It's Too Easy: Just boot the computer with a boot disk that is _not_ set up to start the DOS Shell automatically. Then use **DIR**, **TREE**, or **CHKDSK** to find the interesting file(s)—and help yourself.

The moral of the story?

Don't trust menu-dependent password schemes on personal computers for anything more than light protection against inadvertent entry into your files—passwords are too easy to defeat.

_The Un-Commands_*

Wouldn't it be nice to be able to erase files and then get them back—like throwing something in the garbage and then digging it back out? (It might be OK, or it might be ruined, but at least it's a chance.)

DOS 5 has two commands to help you try to retrieve thrown-away files: **UNDELETE** and **UNFORMAT**. Sometimes they can help, sometimes they can't—but at least they give you a shot at untrashing files.

When DOS deletes a file, it doesn't literally erase the information. Instead, it just alters the file's name slightly to signify that the file is "gone." DOS substitutes a certain seldom-used character for the first letter of the filename—the lowercase Greek letter "sigma," or σ (ASCII character number 229). Then, whenever DOS encounters a file whose name begins with σ, it pretends that the file is erased.

To retrieve a file from the "garbage," the **UNDELETE** command just changes the first character of the filename to something besides σ, which makes it a legitimate filename again. If the information denoted by that name is still on the disk (i.e. if it hasn't been overwritten by a new file), you're back in business.

The **UNFORMAT** command works on a similar principle: When DOS formats a used disk, it pretends the files are not there. The **UNFORMAT** command allows you to try to retrieve the original filenames for all such files on the disk.

---

*These commands work only in DOS 5. If you're using an earlier version of DOS, you can skip ahead now to page 203.

In the Can: Delete the **\WORD\PEOPLE\ADDRESS.TXT** file on the *Power* disk, then bring it back.

Dumpster Dive: (Reminder: If you're using removable disks, you must first copy **UNDELETE** to the *Power* disk.) With the *Power* disk in the **A:** drive, enter:

DEL A:\WORD\PEOPLE\ADDRESS.TXT

Next, verify that the file is "gone:" Enter **DIR A:\WORD\PEOPLE**. Now retrieve it, by entering:

UNDELETE A:\WORD\PEOPLE\ADDRESS.TXT

DOS will show you the filename **?DDRESS.TXT** and ask you if you want that file back.* Then it will ask you for the first letter of the filename. Enter an **A**. You can then confirm that the file is restored by entering **DIR A:\WORD\PEOPLE** again.

Is this retrieval technique foolproof? Nope. Although the information in a file marked as "deleted" is not purposely erased, it's not purposely preserved either. DOS ignores the information entirely—as if it were blank and available disk space—and therefore has no qualms about writing information for a new file there. So if a new file has been written over a "deleted" file before you decide to **UNDELETE** it, you've lost that deleted file for good.

*If you were to use special programmer's tools to examine the disk directly, the filename would indeed begin with σ. However, when communicating with you via the normal user screen, DOS shows you a **?** as the first character of the deleted file's name.

The BACKUP and RESTORE Commands

For most file security problems, here's the first best advice:

Never work at your computer longer than a few minutes without saving your work to a disk!

Then, if the power goes out—for whatever silly reason—you've only lost a small amount of work. The best applications programs help you to do these frequent "Save's" by offering that function on a single convenient key.

That will hedge against losses to internal memory (RAM), but what about disk crashes? You must make *back-up copies* of the valuable files on your disks.

But how frequently should you back up your disk files? Well, stop and think about the main data disks you're using for job or school: If they were destroyed *right now,* where would you be? If the answer is, "in deep doo-doo," then you're not backing up your disks properly.

If you don't have a fixed disk, your backup strategy is relatively simple. Just use the **COPY, XCOPY**, or **DISKCOPY** commands to duplicate the files on your data disks. Then if one disk dies—for whatever reason (head crash, magnetic damage, ice cream, etc.), you have the other one.

And for really long, labor-intensive projects—where even the remote possibility of damaging both the original and the backup disks is intolerable—one backup is not enough! *Make a second backup!*

DOS provides two commands specifically to help you do backups:

BACKUP   copies the files you specify into coded form and places these coded copies into new files on (an)other disk(s). *These files are not directly usable in their new form.*

RESTORE   This command decodes the backup files created by **BACKUP**, restoring them into usable form.

Do This: Make a backup of all files on your *Power* disk—coded on the *Power Backup* disk—with the **BACKUP** command.

Like So: If you have a fixed disk, enter **BACKUP A: B: /S**
If you have only removable disks, find the DOS working disk with the **BACKUP** command. Place it into the **A:** drive and enter* **BACKUP A: B: /S**   Then follow directions (the *Power* disk is the source; *Power Backup* is the target). Then check the result, with a **DIR** of the *Power Backup* disk.... Everything is dumped into one big file, with a "control" file to keep track of it all.

But: You can't use the *Power Backup* files in this form. This is the main difference between **DISKCOPY** and **BACKUP**.

So: (If you don't have a fixed disk, find the DOS working disk with the **RESTORE** command file on it, and put this into the **A:** drive). Enter* **RESTORE A: B: /S** This time, the *Power Backup* disk is the source, and the *Power* disk is the target.

---

*The **/S** switch tells DOS to include the root's sub-directories—and their files and subdirectories.

> **Caution!** Anytime you use the **BACKUP** command, all of the files previously on the destination disk are erased.

Backing Up Application Programs

Theoretically, then, you could back up an entire fixed disk with the **BACKUP** command (as each removable disk filled up, you would be prompted to insert the next disk). Easy, right?

Wrong. How many floppy disks would this take for an average fixed disk? (Approximately *50* disks.) Do you even *have* 50 disks? Do you have the *time* to *insert* 50 disks while they fill up? Are you thinking of converting your computer to a footstool?

You can protect your fixed-disk files more easily than that—just by thinking.

Take, for example, the application program files on your fixed disk. Do these *really* need to be backed up? You probably obtained them on removable disks in the first place—and you *should* have those original disks stored away someplace. Those original disks constitute your backups!

So a large part of your fixed disk doesn't need to be backed up.

Backing Up Data Files

So all *you* need to back up are your data files—and only those you've *changed* since the last time you backed up.

Now, think about tree structures, again: If you keep your data files in certain directories, you need only back up those directories. And remember the **XCOPY** command and how it copies *directories*?...

Mission: To design a system for backing up the word processing files on a fixed disk.

Strategy: Keep these files in a certain directory. Then periodically use the **XCOPY** command to back up this directory to a removable disk, such as your *Power Backup* disk.

===

Then: Pretend you've been working in the **\WORD\PEOPLE** directory. Now efficiently back up all the files in that directory.

1:      *Set the Archive bits* for the files you want to back up—all the files in the directory. Put the *Power* disk into the **A:** drive and enter **ATTRIB +A \WORD\PEOPLE*.*** to mark the files.

2:      Put the *Power Backup* disk into the B: drive (if any); or put the *Power Backup* disk into the A: drive when directed to by DOS. Now enter **XCOPY \WORD\PEOPLE*.* B: /M**

This is when and why you would use the Archive bit in a file's attribute byte (recall pages 198-199).

That **/M** switch used here then modifies the **XCOPY** command so that it will copy only those files (specified) whose Archive bits are set. Then it clears (turns off) those Archive bits.

This approach greatly simplifies your backup process—especially when the files you're copying will occupy multiple floppy disks:

With **XCOPY** and the **/M** switch, the copying just stops after each removable disk fills up, allowing you to put in another backup disk and reissue the **XCOPY.../M** command (and remember that F3 can save you a lot of retyping).

Since the files which were just copied to the previous disk have their Archive bits already cleared at that point, DOS won't copy them to the next disk; it will seek out those files whose Archive bits are still set.

Note: If you ever have a situation where **XCOPY** doesn't work, it may be that you have a file on your fixed disk that is too large to fit on a removable disk. In that situation, you'll have to resort to **BACKUP**, which will split the file onto two or more removable disks.

For example, if you enter **BACKUP C:\DATA**_filename_ **A:**, this will back up just the file called _filename_, instead of the entire disk.

The REPLACE Command

REPLACE is an external command on DOS versions 3.2 and greater (so if you don't have a fixed disk, transfer REPLACE from a DOS working disk to the DOS directory of the *Power* disk).

REPLACE lets you pick and choose which files to back up*—without having to type in all of the file names....

Suppose: You've been working in the \WORD\PEOPLE directory. You've changed some files during the day and you're ready to back them up. How do you ask DOS to give you a list of the files in the directory and *let you easily select individual ones to back up?*

Like This: Put the *Power* disk into the A: drive and the *Power Backup* disk into the B: drive (or wait for DOS's cue to switch it into the A: drive).

Enter REPLACE \WORD\PEOPLE*.* B: /P

The /P switch stands for Prompt—DOS prompts you before replacing each file.

There are some other switches you can use with REPLACE, too. You can read about them in your DOS Manual if you're interested.

---

*REPLACE is handy for updating programs, too: Many large programs use several files—and when such a program is updated by the manufacturer, only some of these files may be changed. The manufacturer can use the REPLACE command to replace only those files.

In Case of Emergency

Sometimes no matter how careful you are, Murphy still wins. There's a classical data disease—usually minor, occasionally disastrous.

The Disease:	<u>**Lost Clusters**</u>

The Symptoms: You get a **Data Recovery Error** when you try to access a file; or,

You get an ominous error message when running **CHKDSK**.

The Cause: When a file is saved to disk, DOS often scatters it over several unattached clusters (recall the discussion on pages 73-74). This is nothing unusual; it's often the most efficient use of disk space. The **F**ile **A**llocation **T**able (**FAT**) then keeps track of the locations of the various parts of the file.

But if the computer loses power—even imperceptibly—during this activity, DOS may not complete it; the contents of the clusters may not match with the FAT. *So you should always exit a program (get back to the DOS prompt) before turning off your computer—to make sure all files are properly saved and recorded in the FAT.*

The Cure(s):
Three of these cures can lead to a fast recovery, but one can be worse than the original disease:

1. *Try Again.* Especially when you get a **Data Recovery error**, try about five times. Sometimes something is slightly out of kilter momentarily but will work itself out on subsequent tries.

2. *Use CHKDSK.* If you get an error from **CHKDSK /V**, DOS will ask if the error should be corrected. Regardless of your answer (give either "yes" or "no") nothing will happen; to repair Lost Clusters with **CHKDSK**, you must use the **/F** (Fix) switch: **CHKDSK /F**.

Then, when you get the error message, answer "yes," and the Lost Clusters will be fixed. They will be put into a separate file named **FILE????.CHK**. You can examine this file (e.g. with **TYPE**) and/or **REN**ame it or append it to the original file.

3. *Use* **RECOVER**. If you know which file is in disarray, the **RECOVER** command usually cures the problem. For example: **RECOVER PHONE.TXT**

4. **RIP**—**R**ecover **I**n a **P**ile. Do this demonstration to see how dangerous this procedure can be:

First, use **DISKCOPY** to back up the *Power* disk to the *Power Backup* disk. Now suppose that *Power Backup* disk has Lost Clusters. Put it into the **A:** drive and enter **RECOVER A:** ....

...The *entire disk* (instead of maybe just the one sick file) is now being recovered. Now enter **DIR** to see the resulting mess. The tree has been destroyed and all of the files have been renamed to numbers.

Can you imagine doing this to a fixed disk? You would spend hours, if not days, straightening out the mess. Yikes!

So **RECOVER** an entire disk *only as a last resort*. Sometimes, it's your only option—may it never happen to you.

<u>**Bottom Line**</u>: Back up your fixed disk regularly!

Safety Inspection

1. How often should you save your files? Back them up?

2. If you **COPY** a file onto another file, is the second file lost?

3. What does a virus do to your computer?

4. What can make the keyboard freeze?

5. How do *write-protection* and *copy-protection* differ?

6. What is an Attribute byte?

7. In the **\WORD\PEOPLE\TODO.TXT** file, is the Archive bit set? If not, clear it.

8. Why aren't passwords foolproof on personal computers?

9. What's the most obvious way of backing up a fixed disk? Why is this method not really any good?

10. What's the difference between **DISKCOPY** and **BACKUP**?

11. Should you back up every file on a fixed disk?

12. What does a tree structure have to do with backing up files?

13. How is the **REPLACE** command like the **COPY** command?

14. How can you get DOS to list all of the files in the **\WORD\PEOPLE** directory, so that you can pick and choose which ones you want to back up—without having to type all of their filenames)?

15. While trying to access the **\123\JOHN0001.TXT** file, you get **Data Recovery error**

    a. What do you do first?

    b. How does **CHKDSK** help you?

    c. What if **CHKDSK** doesn't solve the problem?

    d. What would you probably *not* do in this situation?

Inspection Report

1. You should *save* your files (to disk) every 10-15 minutes when working on your computer. You should *back up* these disk files (i.e. on other disks) whenever you have enough new data to amount to a disaster if your lose it—say, after each work session.

2. Yes, the second file is *overwritten* by the first one—gone forever. *And DOS **does not warn you** before doing this.*

3. A *virus* is a piece of software which lurks, hidden and inert until activated—at a certain or random time, when a file is copied, or when some other particular event happens. When activated, most viruses disrupt RAM and/or erase files on fixed disks.

4. The keyboard freezes up usually when a program goes awry in memory. The only cure is to reboot, often causing data loss.

5. ***Write protection*** prevents a disk from physically receiving files. On a floppy disk, you cover the notch on the edge of the disk. On a microdisk, you slide a small plastic tab forward on one corner of the disk.

   Copy protection makes it difficult to copy a program from the disk. One way to do this is to put an odd-sized sector on the disk.

6. Each disk file has an Attribute byte which tells DOS certain things about the file. Typically, you can adjust only two of the bits on the Attribute byte: You can set the Read-only bit of the Attribute byte to prevent a file from being erased or changed. You can set the Archive bit to mark the file for copying with **XCOPY**.*

   DOS sets the Hidden bit in the **IO.SYS** and **MSDOS.SYS** files so that they don't appear in directories.

7. With the *Power* disk in the **A:** drive, enter **ATTRIB \WORD\PEOPLE\TODO.TXT**.

   You won't see an **A**, indicating that the Archive bit is not set. So enter **ATTRIB +A \WORD\PEOPLE\TODO.TXT** to set the bit.

8. Passwords are generally not foolproof on personal computers because a knowledgeable person can boot the computer with his/her own boot disk and bypass any password requests.

9. The most obvious way to back up a fixed disk is simply to enter **BACKUP C: A: /s** This would copy the entire fixed disk onto some 50 or more removable disks. But most people in their right minds aren't going to waste hours inserting 50 disks one after the other. Better methods are suggested throughout this chapter.

---

*If you're running DOS 5, you can also change the Hidden and System bits of the Attribute byte.

10. Both **DISKCOPY** and **BACKUP** transfer information from one disk to another. With **DISKCOPY**, the second disk is exactly the same as the first; it can be used immediately. But with **BACKUP**, the second disk is in a code; you must use the **RECOVER** command to decode these files.

11. Generally speaking, you're wasting your time if you back up program files on fixed disks. Even if the fixed disk is erased, you should still have the manufacturer's original disks; they can act as your backups.

12. You should make frequent backups only of the files you're currently using. So put each project in a separate directory of your disk tree—and dedicate a backup floppy (or micro) disk as a backup disk for each project. Then, whenever you work on a project, just back up its directory to the corresponding removable disk. This makes backing up easy; you can do it several times a day with no hassle.

13. **REPLACE** and **COPY** both use the same general form when their commands are entered:

    REPLACE *Source Destination*

    COPY *Source Destination*

14. With the *Power* disk in the **A:** drive and the *Power Backup* disk in the **B:** drive (if any), enter:

REPLACE \WORD\PEOPLE*.* B: /P.

The **/P** stands for Prompt. DOS will present you with a list of all of the files in the directory. Each file you select will be backed up to the other disk.

15. You can try several things to save the **\123\JOHN0001.TXT** file—in this order:

a. First, try repeatedly to access the file. You might get lucky.

b. If plan **a** doesn't work, try **CHKDSK /F**. If **CHKDSK** recognizes the problem with the bad file (it may not), DOS will offer to fix the problem. Go for it.

c. If plan **b** fails, try **RECOVER \123\JOHN0001.TXT**. You probably won't be able to tell if anything actually happened—but don't fret. When the DOS prompt comes back, try to access the file again.

d. You may be tempted to enter **RECOVER A:**. This would probably be inappropriate for this situation because it would mess up *all the filenames* on the disk—a cure probably worse than the disease.

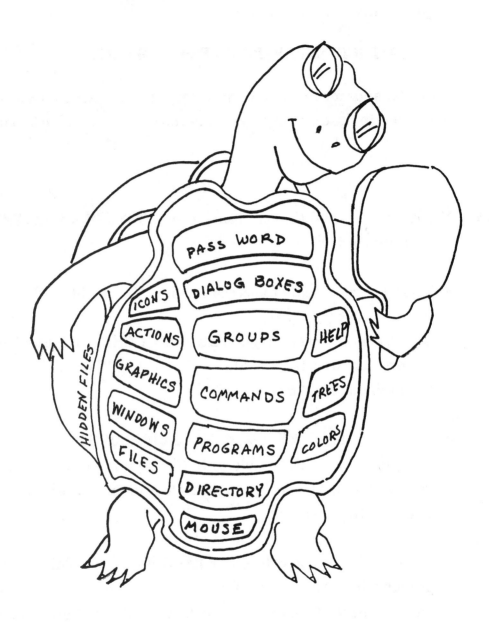

11. USING THE DOS SHELL

What Good Is It?

You've already read a little bit about shells—what they are and why they were created (see pages 116-118 for a refresher).

As you know, the DOS Shell* is a *second-level* shell. It puts a second layer of interpretive "friendliness" between you and the kernel operating system program, `MSDOS.SYS`. Remember that the first layer of shell is the `COMMAND.COM` command interpreter program, which offers you the DOS prompt.

The DOS Shell's main contribution to friendliness is the set of menus it offers. You select items from the menu rather than type in commands. Also, the *Shell* has these other advantages:

- Its windows present a lot of information more *visually*—including the files you want to view.

- Its menus can be customized—even with passwords—to start programs. By customizing the menus, you can depart from the strict tree structure of a disk. The tree is still on the disk, but the menus can organize programs differently.

- It lets you use a mouse.

---

*This chapter is about the MS-DOS 5.0 DOS Shell, which is different than the DOS Shell available in DOS versions 4.0 and 4.01. If you are using DOS 4.0 or 4.01, then read Appendix F instead of this chapter. If you're using a version of DOS earlier than 4.0, then you do not have a DOS Shell at all, so you can just skip to the next chapter.

Learning the Basics

Enough talk. You need some hands on experience with the Shell.

Go: First, to make sure that the **PRINT** command is installed, enter **PRINT** from the DOS prompt. If the resulting message is **Name of list device [PRN]**, just press ⌷←ENTER⌷ to install **PRINT**. If it says **PRINT queue is empty**, **PRINT** is already installed.

Now you can start the DOS Shell: Enter **DOSSHELL**.

Selecting vs. Typing

With the DOS prompt, you must memorize the commands and type them; if you don't know the commands, you can't use them. The alternative is to *select* commands from a *menu*.

The DOS Shell offers two ways to do this: With a ***mouse***, you select an item on the screen by "pointing" to it and clicking a mouse button.* One click highlights an item; a quick double-click selects it. Without a mouse, you use *keys* (⌷F10⌷, ⌷TAB⌷, and the arrow keys) to highlight items on the screen, then ⌷←ENTER⌷ to make your selection. Some people prefer this method since their hands don't leave the keyboard, but it makes screen cursor movement slower and more confusing. Without a mouse, the Shell is often more trouble than convenience.

---

*If your mouse has two or more buttons, you'll use one—the left-hand button—almost exclusively.

11. Using the DOS Shell

Help Windows

Of course, the mouse doesn't have to select everything. Some of the Shell's features _are_ selected more easily with function keys. The first of these, F1, _helps_ you with the rest of the Shell....

Get Help: _Select_ (via mouse or keyboard) **Help** at the top of the screen; or, press F1.

The Help system is _context sensitive._ The Shell makes a good guess as to your problem and offers (usually) the right _window*_ of advice. If its guess is wrong, you can also get an index of all available Help windows.

Try It: Using either mouse or keyboard, select the word **Index** in the first Help window. You have over 30 Help windows, including two special types:

- If you select **Help** from _within_ a Help window, you will see another window that "helps you with Help."

- If you select **Keys** from _within_ a Help window, you will get a special Help window which explains the many ways to use certain keys on the keyboard.

When you've finished with Help, press the ESC key to return to what you were doing before.

---

*A _window_ is simply a boxed-off area of a video screen which contains certain information. Don't confuse this generic term with Microsoft's commercial product, called Windows.®

Double-Dating

The DOS Shell has 4 primary components:

Directory Tree ⎫ File List   Program ⎧**Main**
Directory List ⎭ pair   List pair ⎩**Active Task List**

Each component can have its own window on the video screen. These four "items" fit together in two pairs—like a double date.

So: Be a Matchmaker. Set up the DOS Shell so that both "couples" of the "double date" are visible.

For the File List pair, press F10 to get the overhead menu. Then select **View** and **Program/File Lists**. (If the **Program/File Lists** menu item is dim, it's already selected; press ESC.)

For the Program List pair: If you don't already see the **Active Task List** window in the lower right of the screen, press F10 to get the overhead menu, then select **Options** and **Enable Task Swapper**.

Now you should see the File List pair in the top two windows and the Program List pair in the bottom two windows. Notice that the title of the Directory List (upper right) is the designation of files to be displayed, such as ***.***.

Getting to Know the File List Pair

It's not really a date if you don't go somewhere. And the "double date" of the File List and Program List pairs is no exception. Its destination is a disk.

Start the Date: Designate the *Power* disk as the destination for the "double date."

Here's How: Put the *Power* disk into the **A:** drive.

      At the top of the screen, just under the overhead menu, you'll see a display of the disk drives available to you. It looks something like this:

        [A:] [B:] [C:]

      (Your display may differ, depending upon how many disk drives your system has.)

      Select **[A:]**. This sets the destination of the "double date" to the **A:** drive.

The Directory Tree should now show the tree of the *Power* disk. The Directory List's title is **A:*.***, which tells you which files are being displayed. But instead of a list, there's just a message:

No files in selected directory.

Question: Why don't you see a list of files?

Answer: Because the root directory of the *Power* disk doesn't contain any files right now.

To see a list of the files in the DOS directory of the *Power* disk, just select the word **DOS** in the disk tree (with a mouse, just point and click at **DOS**; otherwise, TAB until one of the directories is highlighted, then use the arrow keys to highlight DOS).... The upper part of your screen shows a list of the files in the DOS directory of your *Power* disk—the DOS commands you've copied there throughout this book—in alphabetical order.

And Look: Select other directories from the disk tree on the left side of the screen. In each case, you'll see an alphabetical listing of that directory's files on the right half of the screen. To get files and directories from another disk, just select **A, B, C**, etc., from the disk drive icons in the upper left part of the screen.

The tree list and the file list are great even when used separately. But when you combine them, you *really* get a lot of power....

Take a closer look at the file list. Each line shows the following:

- The size of the file, in bytes;

- The date when the file was last changed.

Also, notice the ***.*** at the top of the list. As you remember from pages 170-174, this wildcard means "all files in the selected directory." So that's what the file list is currently displaying.

Then, at the right of the file list is a ***scroll bar*** (with arrows at top and bottom), which you can use to move through the files on the screen. That's right—*unlike* the regular **DIR**ectory command (which gives you only one chance to read)—you can easily scroll up and down the file list like this, scanning the entire list back and forth.

Look Around: Can you use the File List pair quickly and easily to flip through the files on your fixed disk?

Piece of Cake: Select the **C** icon to show the tree for your fixed disk. Then select any directory from the tree and get a list of its files on the right side of the screen. Use the scroll bars to move your disk tree and your file lists up and down....

Beats the heck out of the DOS prompt, doesn't it?

Doing Things to Files

Of course, you don't just _look_ at files, you _do_ things with them....

Ready: Make sure the _Power_ disk is in the A: drive. Select the A icon so that the tree for the _Power_ disk is displayed. Then select the **\DOS** directory.

Set: Before you can do something with a file, you have to select one. So, select the **CHKDSK** file (point and click at the **CHKDSK** file with a mouse; or (TAB) and use the arrow keys to highlight **CHKDSK**.)

Go: Press (←ENTER) to start **CHKDSK**. DOS will exit the DOS Shell, execute **CHKDSK**, and return to the DOS Shell. (It may take several seconds to do this.)

This is an easy way to start a program from within the DOS Shell. (In this case, the program is a DOS command, **CHKDSK**). You'll see a more sophisticated way to start files from the Main window—stay tuned.

Honey, I Shrunk the Disk Tree

The display in the Directory Tree window can expand and shrink. If you see a **[+]** symbol, this means there's more than meets the eye; a **[-]** symbol means what is there can be shrunk out of sight; a **[   ]** symbol means nothing can be expanded or shrunk.

For example, look at the Directory Tree for the _Power_ disk. The **WORD** and **EDITLINE** directories have the **[+]** symbol. (You may have to scroll down to see them.)

Expand Things: Highlight **EDITLINE** and press ⊞. Two things will happen: The **JOHN** and **MARY** subdirectories will appear; and the **[+]** will change to a **[-]**.

Shrink Things: Highlight **EDITLINE** and press ⊟. The subdirectories will disappear, and the **[-]** will change back to a **[+]**.

Expand Everything: Go down the Directory Tree and expand every directory marked with **[+]**.

Now you're ready for some file action....

Practice using the File System now, with these tasks....

Task: Print the **SHOP.TXT** file (be sure the printer is on and ready): Select the **\WORD\PEOPLE** directory, then the **SHOP.TXT** file. Select **File** and then **Print**.... Voilá!

Next: Set up the text files so that you can open them with **EDIT**. Select the **C:** drive, the **\DOS** directory, and the **EDIT** file. Then select **File** and **Associate**.

When asked by the dialog window, enter **TXT**. This associates all **.TXT** files with the **EDIT** command. To test this new association, select the **A:** drive, the **\WORD\PEOPLE** directory, and **ADDRESS.TXT**. Press ⌐←ENTER⌐.... See? DOS leaves the DOS Shell and runs **EDIT** with the **ADDRESS.TXT** file loaded.   Exit **EDIT**, and return to the DOS Shell.

Then: Move **EDLIN** from the **\EDITLINE** directory to the **\DOS** directory. Select the **\EDITLINE** directory, then **EDLIN**. Select **File** and **Move**. A dialog window will ask for the destination, so then enter **A:\DOS**. The file is then moved to **\DOS** and erased from **\EDITLINE**—all in one step!

Now: Copy **EDLIN** back to the **\EDITLINE** directory. Select the **\DOS** directory, then select **EDLIN**. Select **File** and **Copy**. A dialog window will ask for the destination, so then enter **A:\EDITLINE**. The file is *copied* to **\EDITLINE**; it also remains in **\DOS**.

Now: Delete **EDLIN** in the **\EDITLINE** directory: First, select the **\EDITLINE** directory, then the **EDLIN** file. Then select **File** and **Delete**. You will be asked to confirm that you really do want to delete the file.

And: Rename the **MEMO.TXT** file to **MEMO2.TXT**: Select the **\WORD\PEOPLE** directory, then the **MEMO.TXT** file. Select **File** and **Rename**. Enter **MEMO2.TXT**; now that's the name.

Then: Make **SHOP.TXT** a *hidden file*: Select **SHOP.TXT**, then **File** and **Change attribute**. Highlight **Hidden**, press the space bar and select **Enter** (or press ←ENTER).

SHOP.TXT is now a hidden file; it will not appear in some **DIR**ectory listings.

Last: Add a **BOB** directory to **\WORD\PEOPLE**: First, move over to **\WORD\PEOPLE** in the Directory Tree. Then select **File** and **Create directory**. Then, in the dialog box, enter **BOB**.

By now, you should be starting to "get the hang" of the Shell's menu-oriented way of managing your files. It's just a matter of selecting the file(s) you want to adjust, and then selecting the things you want to do.

Of course, the Shell can't do everything—but the things it *does* do are as easy as pointing and clicking with a mouse. And there's more....

Options: How Much Help Do You Want?

For more power and convenience, the Shell offers you certain _options_ that affect how the File System displays and handles files.

Hmm: Display the **\WORD\PEOPLE** directory so that only **.TXT** (not **.BAK**) files are displayed—by order of their dates.

Easy: Select **Options** and **File Display Options**. In the dialog box, type ***.TXT** (don't press ⎯ENTER yet) to request all **.TXT** files. Then select **Date** (press TAB if you don't have a mouse). _Now_ press or select ⎯ENTER.... Voilá—less clutter for your (and eyes) without the redundant backup files!

OK: Return to the standard display: Select **Options** and **File Display Options**. Type ***.***; and select **Name**. This displays all files in alphabetical order, as before.

Now: Can you create your own file-handling safety net, by telling DOS to check with you before erasing or overwriting files?

Sure: Select **Options** and **Confirmation**. Now, as you wish, you can turn on or off: **Confirm on delete**
                               Confirm on replace
                               Confirm on Mouse Operation

To change an item, move the cursor to it and press SPACE BAR.*

---

*Recommendation: When moving many files between directories, temporarily turn off the **Confirm on replace** option, so you won't spend all day confirming file after file, ad nauseam.

Arrange: The Big Picture

Do you see how the **Options** can help you do your file management work more efficiently? And there's one more powerful option you ought to know.

The **Arrange** option is the best cure for Murphy's Tree Law: "No matter where you put a file, later you'll look for it in another directory."

Quick: What directory on your *Power* disk has the **COPY.TXT** file?

"Uh..." Who knows? It simply isn't possible to remember the exact locations of all your many files. That's where the **Arrange** option comes in handy: Select **View** and **All Files**. Then select **COPY.TXT**.

Now all the files on the *Power* disk are listed alphabetically, regardless of their directories.

Notice, too, the information displayed about the **COPY.TXT** file—its directory, its attribute bits, etc. And to see what's in that file, just select **File** and **View File Contents** (recall that you made **COPY.TXT** on page 168—to practice with **COPY**).

Press [ESC] to stop viewing.

Now, go back to the "double date:" Select **View** and **Program/File Lists**.

Getting to Know the Program List Pair

The second couple on the "double date" is the Menu and the Active Task List—appearing in the lower left-hand and lower right-hand windows, respectively. You use each of them to start ("launch") programs, but under different conditions.

Launch One: Launch the **EDIT** command via the **Editor** menu item in the **Main** window.

3, 2, 1... : Select **Editor** and press (←ENTER).

When asked for a file to edit, press (←ENTER) again. This launches **EDIT** (and it takes a few seconds).

Exit it and return to the DOS Shell.

Starting Your Own Programs

The good news is that you can add any program you want to this menu list. Once you've added it, you can start that program simply by selecting its menu item.

OK: Can you put the **CHKDSK** command into this menu?

Yep: First, tell DOS that you want to add something to the menu: Select **File** and **New**. (Notice that the overhead menu items have changed since you entered the **Main** window.)

Next, select Program Item, and give the program a title: Enter **CHecK DiSK**. So far, so good, but that's just the title—the menu item's appearance in the menu. You still need to tell the Shell what to *do* when that item is selected.

So the next step is to enter the commands: Press TAB to move the cursor to the next line (**Commands**). Tell the Shell how to start the program, by entering these commands:*

CHKDSK /V | MORE

After all, that's what you would enter if you were at the DOS prompt, right?

---

*Cautionary note: Do not use the **CHKDSK /F** switch from within the DOS Shell. It can damage files which the DOS Shell has open.

Is that it? Have you completed the process of adding the command **CHKDSK** as a program on the menu?

Not Quite: You still need to give some details. TAB to the next line in order to enter the **Startup Directory**: Type **C:\DOS**. This is the location of the program, **CHKDSK**.

Now enter a password: Press TAB to get to the password entry, then enter **EC** (for Easy Course). That's now the password for using the new **CHecK DiSK** menu item.

Then end the procedure: Press ←ENTER. **CHecK DiSK** now appears as an item in the **Main** window. Highlight it and press ←ENTER to test it.... It takes a few seconds to run, and then it brings you back to the DOS Shell.

Question: On page 226, you launched the **CHKDSK** command by selecting it from the file list. How does that method compare with this method?

Pros: By putting a program into the **Main** menu you don't have to locate it on the disk; you just select it as a menu item. Also, by setting up a program as a menu item, you can include parameters (e.g. **/V | MORE**)—not possible when launching a program from the Directory List.

Cons: It's quite a rigmarole to put a program on the menu—not worthwhile unless you use the program often.

Groups

Group in the DOS Shell is just another word for *menu*.

The Shell initially has two groups: The **Main** group (Main menu), and the **Disk Utilities** group—a sub-group, since you get to it by selecting an item from the **Main** group. You can tell when a menu item—such as **Disk Utilities...**—does indeed lead to a sub-group (menu) because it's followed by **....**

To see how a group (menu) works, select **Disk Utilities....** You'll get another menu, which consists of DOS commands. Press ESC to return to the Main group (menu).

Challenge: Can you copy the **CHecK DiSK** menu item from the **Main** group to the **Disk Utilities** group?

No Sweat: Highlight **CHecK DiSK**

Select **File**, then **Copy**   (Instructions will appear on the screen.)

Select **Disk Utilities....** (Don't just highlight— actually go to the **Disk Utilities** menu.)

Press F2

The **CHecK DiSK** menu item will be copied to the **Disk Utilities** group. (Scroll down to see it, if necessary.)

Issuing Commands

Did you realize that, without having to add anything to a menu, you can give some commands to DOS from the Shell? And you're already in the right place to do it, too—look at the various menu items in the **Disk Utilities...** group:

> **Disk Copy**
> **Disk Compare**
> **Backup fixed disk**
> **Restore fixed disk**
> **Quick Format***
> **Format**
> **Undelete**

Look familiar? These are just the same old commands you've been reading about—and typing from the DOS prompt. Select one and you'll get a window asking the parameters needed to carry out the command.

Ho Hum: Make a current copy of the *Power* disk.

Nothin' To It: Select **Disk Copy**. Then change the parameters, if necessary—follow the instructions on the screen.

From the **Disk Utilities** menu, press ⌇ESC⌇ to return to the **Main** menu. Oops—**CHecK DiSK** is still there (no sense keeping it there when it's already on the **Disk Utilities** menu). Highlight it and select **File** and **Delete** to clear it from this menu.

*This command does not check for bad areas on the disk.

Task Swapping

"Task swapping" really just means "program swapping"—a way to jump between two or more programs without exiting them. (Only one program actually _runs_ at a time, though—the others are put "on hold.") The Active Task List works much like the Main window, but it lets you swap in this way between programs. Any program on the Active Task List is in "suspended animation."

Challenge: Run **EDIT** and **QBasic**. Set them up so that you can swap between them.

Swap Meet: First, select **Editor** from the **Main** window, then press ⟨←ENTER⟩⟨←ENTER⟩ to launch the **EDIT** command. Inside the Editor, type **Now inside the editor**. Press **CTRL**-⟨ESC⟩ to return to the DOS Shell without exiting the Editor. **Editor** now appears in the **Active Task List** window. It is "frozen in time," awaiting your future actions.

Next, do the same procedure for **QBasic**: Select **QBasic** from the **Main** window and press ⟨←ENTER⟩ ⟨←ENTER⟩ to launch it. Type **Now inside QBasic**. Press **CTRL**-⟨ESC⟩ to return to the DOS Shell. QBasic is now "on ice"—added to the Active Task List.

Now you can easily jump back and forth—swap—between **EDIT** and **QBasic**.

Do the Swap: Select **Editor** from the **Active Task List** (instead of from the **Main** menu). The Editor re-animates—exactly at the point where you left it before. Press CTRL-ESC to return.

Similarly, select **QBasic** from the **Active Task List**. Instantly, it "thaws out" to where you left it previously. Press CTRL-ESC to return.

In this way, you can swap between **Editor** and **QBasic** as often as you wish. And of course, you can add more programs to the Active Task List and swap between them, too.

Swap 'Till You Drop: When you've had enough swapping, select the **Editor** (again, from the **Active Task List**), but this time exit it in the normal manner (*not* via CTRL-ESC). Do the same for QBasic. They'll be removed from the Active Task List.

As you can see, the trick to swapping is to use the key combination CTRL-ESC from within a program. When you do, that program is placed on the Active Task List and thus becomes available for swapping. (Of course, in order for this to work, the program must have been originally launched from within the DOS Shell.)

Shell Game

1. Does the DOS Shell replace the DOS prompt?

2. Can you use the DOS Shell without a mouse?

3. How do you: Start the DOS Shell from the DOS prompt? Find a particular Help screen? Initiate any DOS command in the **Disk Utilities** group?

4. Put **TREE** as an item on the **Main** menu of the DOS Shell. Give it the title **TREE**. Use the **MORE** pipe to pause the display. Use the password **EC2**. Next, test the entry. Finally, copy this new menu item into the **Disk Utilities** group.

5. What's the largest file (in bytes) on the *Power* disk?

6. How can you find all of the **JOHN.TXT** files on the *Power* disk?

7. You **View** a text file; you **Open** a text file. What's the difference?

Watch the Pea

1. The DOS prompt requires you to type in commands; the Shell offers menu items to be selected. But when you execute a DOS command from the Shell, **COMMAND.COM** is still called to do the work. So the DOS Shell *enhances* **COMMAND.COM**—by helping to interpret it—but it does *not* replace it; the Shell does many things well, but it won't do everything the prompt does.

2. It's possible—but not worth the trouble: You use a combination of F10, TAB, and the arrow keys to move around. Phooey.

3. First, the DOS Shell must be installed using the DOS *Install* disk. Once that's done, you can get to the Shell from the DOS prompt by entering **DOSSHELL**.

    To find any particular Help screen in the Shell, press F1 for help, and select **Index**. Then you can select the particular Help screen you want.

    To initiate a command from the **Disk Utilities** group, start a command just as you start a program—double-click it with a mouse, or highlight it and press ←ENTER.

4. Highlight the **Main** window, then select **File**, then **New**, then **Program Item**. For the title, enter **TREE**. (TAB) to the next line (**Commands**), and enter **TREE C:\ | MORE**.

   (TAB) to the **Startup Directory** line, and enter **C:\DOS**. (TAB) to the **Password** line and enter **EC2**—the password. Press (←ENTER).... TREE will be added to the **Main** window.

   To test this new item, select the new **TREE** menu item. When asked for the password, enter **EC2**. The DOS Shell disappears and the **TREE** command takes over.... After **TREE** finishes, you'll return to the DOS Shell.

   To move the **TREE** menu item, first highlight it, then select **File** and **Copy**. Next, go to the **Disk Utilities** menu, and press (F2).... You may have to scroll down to see the result—the new menu item.

   The **TREE** menu item is now in the **Main** menu and the **Disk Utilities** menu. To erase it on the **Main** menu, first press (ESC) to return to Main, then highlight **TREE**, and select **File** and **Delete**. It's history.

5. To find out, select **[A:]** just below the overhead menu. Select **View** and **All Files**, then **Options, File Display Options**, and **Size**.

All of the files on the *Power* disk will then be displayed—smallest to largest—so just go to the bottom of the list to see which is the largest.

6. Select **Options** and **File Display Options**. In the dialog box, enter **JOHN*.TXT**. Now, only **JOHN** text files are displayed. Highlight various ones among these, and you'll see that they're in various directories—because the **JOHN** files were guinea pigs when you practiced other DOS commands.

7. When you **View** a text file, you stay in the Shell's File System; no other program is involved, and no setup is needed. And of course, no changes can be made to the file.

When you **Open** a text file, you actually exit the File System and enter another program—say, **EDIT** or another word processor. Then, of course, the file can be changed. Remember that to do this kind of file opening, you must first set things up with **File** and **Associate**.

Notes (Yours)

12. MAKING BATCH FILES

What Are Batch Files?

Batches are just *bunches of instructions given to a computer all at once.* The first computer batch files were those sets of punched cards that were fed to the big mainframes.

Nowadays, in DOS, a **batch file** *is a series of commands and keywords all listed together (one command per line) in an* **ASCII** *text file—with a* **.BAT** *extension.* This makes it easy to spot—and because it's just a text file, you can create a batch file with **EDLIN** or a word processor.

The beauty of batch files is that they allow you to *customize your computer.* For example, batch files can do these kinds of chores for you:

- Do a series of repetitive tasks;

- Start commonly used programs;

- Find files and words;

- Automatically enter long and complicated DOS commands.

To be sure, batch files aren't quite the same as real programming (you can't use them to create true applications programs—word processors, spreadsheets or games). But they're awfully handy for so many of the mundane things you find yourself doing with single DOS commands.

Of course, a lot of people have already written lots of handy little batch files—and you may want to copy their techniques. But the idea here is to *learn how to do it yourself*—so that you can further transform your computer into your personalized servant....

A Demonstration Batch File

If you're still in the *DOS Shell*, press F3 to get out (the exercises in this chapter all start at the DOS prompt). Be sure that the *Power* disk is in the A: drive—and enter A: to make it the default drive. Now....

Plan Ahead: You should put your batch files into a **BATCH** directory—so you'll always know where they are. So, first enter **MD A:\BATCH** to create this new directory; then **CD \BATCH** to make it the default directory.

Now, try your first batch file. To create it (remember that it's just a text file), use **EDLIN** (so this will be a good refresher on **EDLIN**, too):

Go: Enter these: **EDLIN INFO.BAT**
> **I**
> **CLS**
> **DATE**
> **TIME**
> **VER**
> **MODE 40**
> **PAUSE A 40-column display**
> **MODE 80**
> **REM An 80-column display**
> F6
> **E**

Now look at what these lines instruct DOS to do: The first line, **EDLIN INFO.BAT**, says what to name the file—and where it will go. Since no pathname is specified, the file will go onto the disk in the default drive (**A:**), in the default directory (**\BATCH**).

The **I**, for Insert, is the **EDLIN** command to start the file. After that, here's what each command does:

CLS:	**CL**ears the **S**creen.
DATE:	displays the date and prompts you for a correction.
TIME:	displays the time and requests a correction.
VER:	displays the version of *DOS* which you are using.
MODE 40:	changes the display to 40 columns.
PAUSE:	displays a message and waits until a key is pressed.
MODE 80:	changes the display to 80 columns.
REM:	displays a **REM**ark.

Granted, these lines don't do very useful things, but they demonstrate the general idea of a batch file (and introduce some new DOS commands). The point is, *you could enter this same set of commands—one at a time—from the DOS prompt.* But since they're recorded in a batch file, DOS will run them automatically, one after another!

Notice the F6—the caboose byte—signalling the end of the file (EOF); and the final **E**, for Exit, saves the file to the disk and exits **EDLIN**.

Run It: Since a batch file is an executable file of commands, you need only enter its filename (no need for the **.BAT** extension); the filename is its *keyword:* **INFO**   ...voilá!

Using Variables in a Batch File

Batch file *variables* are symbols that stand in for parameters and other parts of command sentences—just as algebraic variables are symbols that stand in for numbers in equations. They allow you to write the *general* equation, or—in the case of batch files—the *general* program that will be useful in multiple circumstances.

Challenge: Write a batch file to set up **EDLIN**. The keyword will be **EDIT**, followed by the name of the file to be edited (e.g. **EDIT JOHN.TXT**).

Solution: Before plowing into this, consider the steps involved in starting a program such as **EDLIN**: You set the default drive; you set the default directory; you enter the program's keyword and its parameters (if any). Then, when you're finished, you often reset the default directory to the root—ready for the next task.

Now, you should be in the **BATCH** directory in the **A:** drive with the *Power* disk in that drive. Enter these:

```
EDLIN EDIT.BAT
I
A:
CD \DOS
EDLIN %1
CD \
[F6]
E
```

Run It: To see how this batch file works with variables, enter
EDIT \WORD\PEOPLE\PHONE2.TXT

When you enter this command, DOS automatically breaks it into its two parts and assigns each part a variable:

%0   is assigned to the keyword, **EDIT**

%1   is assigned to the first parameter, the file's pathname, **\WORD\PEOPLE\PHONE2.TXT**

Then *DOS uses these variables when carrying out the instructions in the batch file.* Follow along:

A:	makes **A:** the default drive.
CD \DOS	makes **DOS** the default directory.
EDLIN %1	DOS *substitutes* the parameter it assigned for **%1** (above) so now it actually executes **EDLIN \WORD\PEOPLE\PHONE2.TXT**

That leaves you now in **EDLIN**, looking at its ***** prompt. Enter **L** to List the file.... Yep—it's **PHONE2.TXT**. So enter **E** to Exit **EDLIN** and return to DOS—*which is still waiting to finish the batch file:*

**CD **	changes you back to the root directory.
(F6)	ends the batch file and returns you to the DOS prompt.

Did you notice? As the batch file runs, you can see its commands flash by on the screen (to run it again, remember to change the directory back to **BATCH**).

Now, how would you adapt this batch file for *your* word processor (instead of **EDLIN**)? Just make the appropriate changes!

Think through an example: If your word processor program is in the **C:** drive, change the default drive specifier command in the batch file to **C:** instead of **A:**. If your program is in the **WORD** directory, use **CD \WORD** instead of **CD \DOS** in the batch file. And, of course, use the proper keyword for *your* word processor—instead of **EDLIN**.*

Another thing: In the **EDIT.BAT** example, there was no second parameter. If you had had one, you would have used the variable %2. For a third parameter, you would have used %3, etc.—all the way through %9. Thus, a batch file can handle *nine* parameters (plus the keyword variable, %0) at once.

If you need more than nine parameters, you need to tell DOS to "forget about" the %0 variable, by using the **SHIFT** command in your batch file to *shift the variables down one name:*

The value in %0 is lost (DOS "forgets" about it). Then the value in %1 is *renamed* %0; %2 is *renamed* %1, etc. And that leaves %9 open for a new parameter.

So just type **SHIFT** in the batch file, wherever you need it; you can even use it as many times as you wish.

---

*A *WordPerfect* example is given in the quiz at the end of this chapter.

WILDFIND: A Good Batch File Project

One very good use for a batch file is to *find things....*

Challenge: Write a batch file that will find any given word in any text file in any given directory.

Hmmm... that's not a simple problem. You can't search multiple files (i.e., you can't use ***.***) with just the normal **FIND** command; **FIND** works on *one file at a time*.

However, you *can* create a batch file to sequentially *"feed"* to the **FIND** command all the files you specify.

Planning: The keyword will be, say, **WILDFIND** (a **FIND** command that takes wildcards). Here are the variables DOS will identify from the information you give with the **WILDFIND** command:

%0	**WILDFIND**	the keyword
%1	*"word"*	the word you're searching for*
%2	*path****.***	the directory you're looking in.

To write this batch file, then, you'll have to learn how to do *repetitions of commands* within the file—so that you can repeatedly feed text filenames into the **FIND** command. This is going to call for some of the redirection commands that you already know, too. All in all, it's a worthy problem....

---

*Caution: You can't have any **spaces** in the "word" parameter. If you do, DOS will interpret it as two parameters.

The FOR Command

For those repetitive *loops* within batch file, you need to know about the **FOR** command—sometimes called the **FOR/IN/DO** command. Here's how you would use it with **FIND** in your **WILDFIND** batch file:

> **FOR %%F IN (%2) DO FIND %1 %%F**

Here's the command, broken down into its parts:

FOR %%F IN (%2) DO   Essentially, this is saying: "for *each file* **%%F** in the directory **%2**, *do* the following..."

%%F is an **internal** variable that methodically changes its value every time through the loop. You choose the name of this variable—**%%** followed by something else (**F** seems appropriate since this variable is a file).

FIND %1 %%F   Here's the *"doing"* part of the loop: Essentially, this says "**FIND** the word **%1** in the file **%%F**."

Thus, when the batch file enters this **FOR** loop, the *first* file in the given directory will be assigned the name **%%F**, and the **FIND** command will be performed on that file. Then, **%%F** will be changed to the *next* file in the directory and **FIND** will be used on *that* file, etc.—until all the files are searched.

So this **FOR/IN/DO** command extracts the ***.*** files and feeds them *one at a time* to **FIND**! So far, so good....

Problem: If you run this **FOR/IN/DO** command in a batch file by itself, the screen scrolls by too fast to read the results of the command. What can you do?

Hmm.... The **DIR**ectory command had a **/P** switch to pause the display, but the **FIND** command doesn't have such a switch. The **MORE** filter also slows down the display, but it works only with a single **FIND**—and this **FOR** loop performs *many* **FIND** commands, one after another; the screen *does not stop* after each **FIND**.

Solution: *Redirect* the output from the **FIND** commands to a single file. Then, after the entire **FOR** loop search is completed, you can **TYPE** this single output file to the display, using the **MORE** filter to slow down the display.

Use some simple name, such as **TEMP.TXT**, for this temporary output file.*

---

*Reminder: Whenever you name a file **TEMP.TXT** or something similar, be sure that it is indeed used only for temporary and non-important information!

As you can tell, anytime you ask your computer to do something repetitively, you need to make sure you correctly envision exactly what's going to happen each time through the cycle. *And,* you must leave the environment properly organized at the *end* of each cycle so that the next time around will operate as you expect it to.

For example, with **WILDFIND**, what happens each time the **FIND** is successful? It sends some output to the **TEMP.TXT** file. And then the next time it **FIND**s something and ships it to the **TEMP.TXT** file, will it *overwrite* the previous one or will it add onto it? Add onto it, right? So when you send the output of the **FIND** command to the **TEMP.TXT** file, you need to use the **>>** (*appending*) redirection command.

All right, now suppose that **WILDFIND** has successfully looked through all the files in the given directory, found a few occurrences of its target word, shipped these results to the **TEMP.TXT** file (appending in each occurrence), etc. The question now is: What will happen the next time you run **WILDFIND**—looking for a completely different word?

If the **TEMP.TXT** file is still filled with the search results from last time, your results from this time will just be appended below those previous results, right? Looks as if you'd better *empty* the **TEMP.TXT** file before using it—like taking out yesterday's garbage—right?

Problem: Find a way to erase **TEMP.TXT** in **WILDFIND**.

Solution: You *could* use the command **ERASE TEMP.TXT**, but then, what if the **TEMP.TXT** file doesn't yet exist? Suppose somebody else has already taken out the garbage—or suppose this is your first use of **WILDFIND** in the default directory? If you try to erase a file that doesn't exist, you'll get an error message, clutter up the screen and stop the execution of the batch file! Not so good.

Well, DOS provides a way to check for the existence of a file: **IF EXIST**. Here's how you would use it:

IF EXIST TEMP.TXT ERASE TEMP.TXT

Essentially this command says: "If **TEMP.TXT** exists, then **ERASE TEMP.TXT**; if not, *do nothing*."

All right—that's another little hassle taken care of.

See any others?...

One more thing: When a batch file runs, it can produce a lot of unnecessary clutter on the screen. Normally, when you give DOS a command, it echoes it onto your monitor (it doesn't *have* to do that, you know—it's just to let you see what you've typed).

But you can turn this echo off when you want to run a set of commands at once—in a batch file: **ECHO OFF** doesn't turn off everything in the display—just the commands. The *results* of the commands (and any error messages) *are* displayed.

Problem: You can use **ECHO OFF** in your batch file, all right, but that very command will be displayed before it has a chance to take effect. How can you prevent this?

Solution: Use **@ECHO OFF**. **@** hides the echo of any single line of a batch file (available only on DOS versions 3.3 and later.

You should know that **ECHO** has another function....

Try This: Enter **ECHO Hey, Dude!**

Result: **Hey, Dude!** appears on the screen.

ECHO alone *will display messages on the screen*—with *either* **ECHO ON** or **ECHO OFF**. By contrast, **REM**ark won't display a message with **ECHO OFF**. So use **ECHO** for messages that must always be displayed; use **REM**arks as **REM**inders for persons writing (or reading) the batch file.

Now, *finally*, you've considered and planned for—the little annoyances, and you're ready to write the actual batch file, **WILDFIND.BAT**....

Write It:
```
EDLIN A:\BATCH\WILDFIND.BAT
I
ECHO OFF
ECHO Searching...
IF EXIST TEMP.TXT ERASE TEMP.TXT
FOR %%F IN (%2) DO FIND %1 %%F >>TEMP.TXT
TYPE TEMP.TXT | MORE
F6
E
```

Run It: Enter these:

```
CD A:\BATCH
WILDFIND "Grapevine" A:\WORD\PEOPLE\*.*
```

You'll soon see a list of all lines containing **Grapevine** in all text files in the **\WORD\PEOPLE** directory. Here's what happens during **WILDFIND**, line by line:

ECHO OFF keeps the commands from being displayed.

ECHO Searching... displays a diversion message.

IF EXIST TEMP.TXT ERASE TEMP.TXT erases **TEMP.TXT**—if it already exists.

FOR %%P IN (%2) DO FIND %1 %%P >>TEMP.TXT searches the files and places the results in **TEMP.TXT**.

TYPE TEMP.TXT | MORE shows you the search results —one screen at a time!

WILDFIND: A Good Batch File Project

DOS Environment Variables

Just so you know: The third type of batch file variable you can use is called an **environment variable.** The DOS *environment* is a small area of memory set aside for these variables.

Do This: Enter **SET**

You'll see what variables are currently stored in your DOS environment—maybe a **COMSPEC** (COMmand SPECification) variable, which tracks the location of your **COMMAND.COM** file. You'll also see a **PATH** variable and— if you still have a customized prompt—a **PROMPT** variable.

But you can put your own variables in the DOS environment, too....

Try It: Enter **SET EC=Easy Course**. Then enter **SET**, and you should see **EC** as a new variable.

The point is, your batch files can use any of these variables. To refer to them, you just enclose them with % signs. For example, to display the contents of your new **EC** variable, the line to include in a batch file would be: **ECHO The EC variable is %EC%.**

Then, when you ran the completed batch file, you'd see this on your screen:

The EC variable is Easy Course.

A Batch of Questions

1. Batch files consist of what two types of things?

2. What's the difference between programs and batch files?

3. Batch files must have what kind of filename extension? Are batch files program, data, or text files?

4. Describe the three types of batch file variables.

5. Some programs leave your display in a 40-column mode instead of an 80-column one (not too polite). So write a batch file, named **RESET**, that returns your screen to 80 columns.

6. When you start a sophisticated program, you often need to set the disk drive, and set the directory. After the program is terminated, you want to return the directory to the root. Batch files are ideal for this. Set up a batch file to start *WordPerfect*. Name the batch file **PERFECT**.

7. Write a batch file that starts automatically when you boot the computer.

A Batch of Answers

1. Batch files consist of commands and keywords.

2. Programs have the sophistication needed for word processors, spreadsheets, and games. Batch files are limited to what keywords and DOS commands can do.

3. Batch files are text files. They must have a **.BAT** filename extension.

4. The three types of batch file variables are:

   Parameter variables. Example: **%1**. These are the variables assigned to the parameters and keyword (name) of your batch file. There are just ten possible parameter variables (**%0, %1, %2,... %9**), each preceded by a single **%**.

   FOR/IN/DO *variables.* Example: **%%F**. These are the variables you use within **FOR** commands to represent the "loop counters." They are preceded by **%%**.

   DOS environment variables. Example, **%PATH%**. These variables "live" out in the DOS environment—and you can name them and give them values to be used within your batch files. These variables are always enclosed in **%**'s.

5. With the *Power Disk* in the A drive, enter:

```
A: CD \BATCH
EDLIN RESET.BAT
I
MODE 80
[F6]
E
```

As you can tell here, the actual batch file consists of just one line (MODE 80). This is an example of customizing a batch file to rename commands: If you can't remember MODE 80, no sweat. Just enter RESET—or name it anything that you'll remember.

6. Do this exercise only if you have the *WordPerfect* program on a fixed disk (installed in a directory called \WP). If you don't have that program, just read along here—and consider using this same general pattern to set up the application programs you *do* have:

```
EDLIN \BATCH\PERFECT.BAT
I
```

@ECHO OFF   turns off the background clutter (without DOS version 3.3 or later, omit the @).

ECHO Loading WordPerfect... keeps you informed while the program is loaded from the disk.

C: moves DOS to the correct drive.

CD \WP   moves DOS to the correct directory.

WP %1 starts the *WordPerfect* program. The **%1** represents the filename parameter you'll also supply when you invoke **PERFECT** (e.g. **PERFECT THISFILE.WPF**).*

ECHO Leaving WordPerfect... keeps you informed as the program closes and quits; there are several seconds between the time a file closes and the DOS Shell returns.

CD ** returns you to the root of the disk tree so that you don't accidentally try to start your next program from the **\\WP directory.

F6

E

7. DOS offers you a specially-named batch file, **AUTOEXEC.BAT**, which runs automatically every time you boot the computer. Writing this file is a topic for the next chapter ...

---

*The .WPF extension stands for WordPerfect File.

Notes (Yours)

13. PUTTING IT ALL TOGETHER

Customizing DOS for *You*

Your personal computer arrives unadorned and rather impersonal, actually. To make it right for you, you need to add a few personal touches—*customize* it for your own work needs and style. And nobody but *you* can do this. After all, you don't let anyone else dress you or arrange your desk. Why should you let a friend or dealer "dress" your computer or arrange your disk?

This isn't going to mean learning a lot of new commands or concepts. Indeed, you've already seen most of the customizable features of DOS:

- You can make your own tree;

- You can write your own batch files;

- You can customize the DOS prompt.

Now it's just a matter of putting it all together.

But first you'd better decide what you want to do—and it's more than just adding a few frills here and there. You need an overall plan with some coordinated goals:

- Configure your computer system to handle a variety of application programs without needing frequent changes.

- Have the computer perform some mundane tasks automatically every time it is booted.

- Design a logical, organized tree structure on your fixed disk.

These are the goals of this chapter....

CONFIG.SYS: Your System Settings

The first chance you have to adjust your computer is in a special file called **CONFIG.SYS** ("CONFIGure SYStem").

A **CONFIG.SYS** file—if it exists (it's *not* essential; DOS will boot and run without it)—must be located in *the root directory of the disk you use to boot your computer.*

Question: Do you already have a **CONFIG.SYS** file? How do you find out?

Answer: If you have a fixed disk, enter **TYPE C:\CONFIG.SYS**. Or, put the removable boot disk you normally use into the **A:** drive and enter **TYPE A:\CONFIG.SYS**.

If you have a **CONFIG.SYS** file, it will be displayed on the screen; if not, you'll see **File not found**.

If you do have a **CONFIG.SYS** file already, you may be wondering where it came from. First of all, DOS version 4.00 or later creates a **CONFIG.SYS** file for you during the installation process. Also, some application programs write a **CONFIG.SYS** file for you (erasing any **CONFIG.SYS** file you already have—an outrageous presumption). Or, a dealer or friend may have written one for you.

But no matter how it got there, wouldn't you rather put together your own **CONFIG.SYS** file—one that reflects your own needs?

CONFIG.SYS is an **ASCII** text file—but it's *not* a batch file. It's a *list of internal settings* for your computer. You can mix and match these settings to fit your needs. Here are four of the more common settings:

BREAK=ON   This setting lets you interrupt (break into) programs while they're running, using `CTRL` `BREAK` or `CTRL` `C`, something that programmers and technicians often need to do.

When a program is "listening" to the keyboard—expecting you to press a key—DOS will watch every keystroke for a `CTRL` `BREAK`. But some programs go a long time without expecting any keyboard input from you, so meanwhile there's no way to interrupt them—without the **BREAK** feature:

When **BREAK=ON**, DOS checks for `CTRL` `BREAK` *even when the program is not expecting keyboard input*. When **BREAK=OFF**, DOS checks for `CTRL` `BREAK` only when the program *is* expecting keyboard input.

FILES=20   This limits how many files your computer can handle at the same time (20 here). File-hungry programs will notify you in their manuals if they need more (very few do). Just set it to 20, or the highest number needed, and leave it there.

FCBS=20,8   Some programs use File Control BlockS (**FCBS**) to handle files. The definition of **FCBS** is technical and not interesting to non-system-programmers. Just take it as a given that this setting is appropriate.

BUFFERS=20   A *buffer* is a part of the computer's memory where disk files are stored *temporarily*. This is why sometimes DOS is able to access a disk without actually using the disk. The wanted file is already in a buffer. With the right number of buffers, this speeds up the computer. Buffers, however, raid memory like teenagers raid the refrigerator—voraciously. If you set BUFFERS too high, it actually slows things down.

Now, knowing just that much about those few system settings,...

Do This: Set up a **CONFIG.SYS** file on the *Boot* disk which sets the above four features.

Solution: Copy **EDLIN** to the *Boot* disk. Then, with the *Boot* disk in the **A:** drive, enter:

```
EDLIN A:\CONFIG.SYS
I
BREAK=ON
FILES=20
FCBS=20,8
BUFFERS=20
F6
E
```

So, is this **CONFIG.SYS** ready to run? *No*—the file is not "runable" like a batch file. *The next time you boot your computer,* these settings will be activated. That's the only way to do it.

And just so you know, here are some other settings you may find in **CONFIG.SYS** files:

SHELL=C:\DOS\COMMAND.COM

This tells DOS where the **COMMAND.COM** file is located (unnecessary if **COMMAND.COM** is in the root directory).

LASTDRIVE=E

This tells DOS the maximum number of disk drives you intend to use. If none is specified, drive **E:** is the highest possible drive.

DEVICE=C:\DOS\RAMDRIVE.SYS 65536
DEVICE=C:\DOS\ANSI.SYS

These are examples of DOS *device installations*. The first one establishes an imaginary 64K disk *in the computer's memory* (a "RAMdrive"). The second one sets up a device called **ANSI.SYS** which controls aspects of the keyboard and screen. The point here is, you can install other devices (e.g. a mouse) in your **CONFIG.SYS** as you add to your system.

DRIVPARM=/D:1/S:9/T:80

If you replace a floppy disk drive with a microdisk drive, you may have to tell DOS about the **_drive parameters_** of the new disk. **/D:1** means *Drive 1* (the **B:** drive; *Drive 0* is the **A:** drive); **/S:9** means 9 Sectors per track; **/T:80** means 80 tracks per side.

Using Your **AUTOEXEC.BAT** File

The **AUTOEXEC.BAT** file is a specially-named batch file (which you can create) that runs automatically every time the computer is booted.

The **AUTOEXEC.BAT** file suffers from some of the same disrespect as the **CONFIG.SYS** file:

- The computer doesn't *have* to have one;
- DOS versions 4.00 and later create one for you;
- Some programs replace *your* file with *their* file (grrr...);
- Your friend or dealer sometimes make one "for you."

So here's another way to take control of your computer and customize it—tailor your **AUTOEXEC.BAT** file to fit *your* needs....

Mission: Create an **AUTOEXEC.BAT** file on the *Boot* disk which will turn on **VERIFY**, put the **PRINT** command into memory (where it will be readily available), change the prompt to **What's new, guru?**, and clear the screen.

Prepare: You'll need to copy **PRINT** to the root directory of the *Boot* disk (do this now).

Then, with the *Boot* disk in the **A:** drive, erase the **AUTOEXEC.BAT** file you made earlier (enter **ERASE A:\AUTOEXEC.BAT**). Finally, check that **A:** is the default drive and that the root is the default directory.

Action: Enter: **EDLIN AUTOEXEC.BAT**
                                    I
                                    @ECHO OFF
                                    ECHO Booting...
                                    VERIFY ON
                                    PRINT /D:PRN > NUL
                                    CLS
                                    PROMPT What's new, guru?$_
                                    ⌷F6⌷
                                    E

@ECHO OFF turns off the screen's command-echo clutter.

ECHO Booting... displays a simple message so that you know your **AUTOEXEC.BAT** file is executing.

VERIFY ON tells DOS to double-check any file it copies, to verify that the copy was actually made.

PRINT /D:PRN > NUL *installs the* **PRINT** *command* in memory (RAM), so that it's ready for action. The **/D:PRN** specifies the **PR**i**N**ter as the destination device for that command. **> NUL** gets rid of unwanted installation messages.

CLS clears the screen.

PROMPT What's new, guru?$_** establishes your customized prompt. The **$_ sends the cursor to the next line.

---

*PRINT will normally display a message that it is being installed. **>** **NUL** stifles the message, by sending it the "null" device. This is just another way of reducing clutter on the screen.

You now have a fairly sophisticated *Boot* disk.

Test It: With the *Boot* disk in the **A :** drive, press the reset button (if any) or press **CTRL** **ALT** **DEL** (together) to soft-boot your computer.

Your *Boot* disk now makes these six contributions to the boot process:

1. A boot record, in the first sector of the disk, advises DOS that this is a boot disk.

2. The **IO.SYS** file, hidden, loads the **BIOS**.

3. The **MSDOS.SYS** file, also hidden, loads the DOS kernel.

4. **CONFIG.SYS** configures the computer to your specifications.

5. **COMMAND.COM** brings you the DOS prompt.

6. **AUTOEXEC.BAT** performs those mundane tasks you just gave it.

You've come a long way—but, your customizing isn't finished yet. Maybe you have a clock or a mouse to prepare....

CLOCK   Some computers must request the time and date every time they are booted—what a bother! But maybe you have a *clock card*—a circuit board inside the computer with a built-in clock and battery. By giving the keyword in your **AUTOEXEC.BAT** file, you can load a program into memory that will then read to DOS the time and date off the clock, thus relieving you of the duty.

The keyword used here is **CLOCK**, *but the keyword for your particular clock program may be different.*

MOUSE   If you have a mouse, then you need some type of device driver software to operate it. You simply invoke its keyword to load this driver program into memory. And you can do this automatically by putting the keyword of that program into your **AUTOEXEC.BAT** file.

The keyword used here is **MOUSE**, *but the keyword for your particular mouse program may be different.*

So, can you guess what your next challenge might be?...

Challenge:	Have your *Boot* disk automatically load the **PRINT**, **CLOCK**, and **MOUSE** programs (if you have them) into memory
Solution:	Copy your **CLOCK** and **MOUSE** programs (if any) to the *Boot* disk. Also, erase your current **AUTOEXEC.BAT** file. Then, enter:

```
EDLIN A:\AUTOEXEC.BAT
I
@ECHO OFF
ECHO Booting ...
VERIFY ON
PRINT /D:PRN > NUL
CLOCK > NUL
MOUSE > NUL
CLS
PROMPT Wizard at work$_
[F6]
E
```

If you *don't* have a fixed disk, this should do the trick—you now have a practical sample of a customized *Boot* disk. Back it up to the *Boot Backup* disk (use **DISKCOPY**), and use it from now on to boot your computer (and you may skip ahead to page 283, if you wish).

If you *do* have a fixed disk, you have some more work to do...

Part 1: Set up a directory structure on your fixed disk that will coordinate with an **AUTOEXEC.BAT** file in efficiently booting your computer.

Solution: You'll need three special directories on your fixed disk:

- **C:\DOS** This directory should already be present on your fixed disk. It contains the DOS files.

- **C:\BATCH** This directory should contain all the batch files you create (except for **AUTOEXEC.BAT**, which should be in the root directory). If you don't already have **\BATCH**, enter **MD C:\BATCH**.

- **C:\UTILITY** This directory should contain the **CLOCK** and **MOUSE** programs (and other similar utility drivers). If you don't already have this directory, enter **MD C:\UTILITY** to make it. Then copy **CLOCK**, **MOUSE**, and any other similar programs into it.

A Bright Idea:

Keep a *copy* of your **AUTOEXEC.BAT** file in the **UTILITY** directory (enter **COPY C:\AUTOEXEC.BAT C:\UTILITY**)*—just in case some smart-aleck new applications program overwrites the **AUTOEXEC.BAT** file in your root directory. Do this now, before the next example.

*Put a copy of **CONFIG.SYS** there, too.

Part 2: Write an **AUTOEXEC.BAT** file that takes full advantage of your fixed disk organization and DOS commands.

Solution: Enter:

```
C:\DOS\EDLIN C:\AUTOEXEC.BAT
I
@ECHO OFF
ECHO Booting...
C:\UTILITY\CLOCK > NUL
PATH C:\DOS;C:\BATCH;
VERIFY ON
FASTOPEN C: > NUL
GRAPHICS
GRAFTABL > NUL
PRINT /D:PRN > NUL
C:\UTILITY\MOUSE > NUL
MIRROR C: /TA /TC
DOSKEY
SET DIRCMD=/A /O /P
SET TEMP=C:\TEMP
CD \
CLS
PROMPT $P$G
DOSSHELL
F6
E
```

Now, admittedly, there are few commands here that you've probably never seen before—and many that you have. So take a look at the newcomers, one at a time....

C:\UTILITY\CLOCK > NUL installs your **CLOCK** program into memory (sending the installation message to the ozone). Of course, if you don't have a **CLOCK**, don't include this line.

PATH C:\DOS;C:\BATCH; defines two search paths—leading to the **\DOS** and **\BATCH** directories. If DOS doesn't find a command or keyword in the default drive and directory, it will next look in **\DOS** and **\BATCH**. This means you can invoke any DOS command or batch file from any directory on the disk.*

FASTOPEN C: > NUL (DOS versions 3.3 and later) keeps a memory table of frequently used file locations, speeding up fixed disks.

GRAPHICS This command loads the **GRAPHICS** command into memory—needed by DOS to **PRINT SCREEN** on a graphics display or printer (this might be irrelevant to you—you judge).

GRAFTABL > NUL (DOS versions 3.0 and later) allows the display of **ASCII** characters with values over 127 on some monitors.

C:\UTILITY\MOUSE > NUL installs your **MOUSE** program (just as the **CLOCK** program was installed a few lines earlier). Include this line only if you have a mouse.

(cont.)

---

*You may wish to add more paths to the **PATH** from time to time. But keep in mind that the **PATH** command works only for executable files (such as programs)—those with **.EXE**, **.COM** and **.BAT** extensions. The **APPEND** command sets paths for *all other files*. **APPEND** is available only in DOS versions 3.2 and greater. Example: **APPEND C:\DATA** (**DATA** being a directory holding data files). However, **APPEND** is *not recommended*; in practical usage, it has been found to scatter data files throughout the directories of a fixed disk.

MIRROR C: /TA /TC creates a "mirror"—a copy—of the **FAT** (File Allocation Table) and directory structure of the **C:** drive, so that the **UNFORMAT** command will work more often. Then the **/TA** and **/TC** switches tell DOS to "Track the **A:** drive" and "Track the **C:** drive," so that file deletions are more easily recovered via **UNDELETE**. Keep in mind that **MIRROR, UNFORMAT**, and **UNDELETE** are available only in DOS 5.

DOSKEY installs a small editor for typing commands at the DOS prompt—available only for MS-DOS 5.0.

SET DIRCMD=/A /O /P automatically invokes the **/A /O /P** switches (see pages 140-141) whenever you use the **DIR** command. **SET DIRCMD** is available only in MS-DOS 5.0.

SET TEMP=C:\TEMP means that anytime DOS creates a temporary file (which it does, for example, every time a pipe is used), the temporary file will be placed in the designated directory. This reserves enough disk space for the temporary file (if a removable disk is a default, it might be too full, causing an error); and it puts all temporary files in one place—where you know they're temporary and can be erased later. (Note that the designated directory, **C:\TEMP**, must actually exist. To make it, enter **MD C:\TEMP**.)

DOSSHELL is the keyword to start the DOS Shell (but note that instead of **DOSSHELL**, you could substitute here the keyword of any program you wanted to start automatically at boot-up.)

OK, does your sophisticated **AUTOEXEC.BAT** file work—coordinating with your fixed-disk directory structure for a good, efficient boot-up?

Test It: Reboot your computer (with the **A:** drive empty).... Your computer should be customized according to those specifications you just spelled out in the **AUTOEXEC.BAT** file.

Something wrong? Delete **@ECHO OFF** and the **> NUL**'s while searching for errors in your **AUTOEXEC.BAT** file. That way, you can see what's going on. When everything's hunky-dory, add them back in.

OK, here's where you must take over: You have your previous **AUTOEXEC.BAT** file stored in the **\UTILITY** directory. You now have this new-and-awesome practice **AUTOEXEC.BAT** file in the root directory.
                   Which do *you want* for your disk?

It's probably a combination of the two—right?

So examine your old **AUTOEXEC.BAT** file to see what's different from your new file. Then decide which commands in the old file you want to incorporate into your new file and use **EDLIN** to make the changes in your new file. Change only one line at a time and then reboot—so that you know each new change actually works.

Then, when you're satisfied, make a copy of the final **AUTOEXEC.BAT** file for the **\UTILITY** directory.

_Planning for Help_*

You may need help to set up DOS, but if you set up DOS 5 correctly, it will offer _you_ help—via the **HELP** command.

Suggestions: For removable disks, make the **A:** drive the default (enter **A:**) and place the _Help_ disk in it. With a fixed disk, the **HELP** command is in your **\DOS** directory. This means that you can access it no matter what the defaults—provided that **\DOS** appears in the **PATH** statement in your **AUTOEXEC.BAT** file (see page 276).

To Get Help: Just enter **HELP**, for starters. You get a list of all of the DOS commands.

For help on an individual command, enter **HELP** and the command name. For example, **HELP DIR** offers help on the **DIR** command. Or, you can simply enter the command and the **/?** switch: **DIR /?** You get the same help screen either way.**

*This page applies to DOS 5 only.

**Of course, the DOS help screens are just like the cryptic explanations in the DOS manuals—which is why you still need this book.

13. PUTTING IT ALL TOGETHER

A Logical and Organized Tree Structure

A well-organized fixed disk will save you time and money. But what is good disk management?

Knowing how to make, change and remove directories isn't enough. And though you've already been introduced to some good ideas about directory management (e.g. keeping your DOS commands collected together in a **\DOS** directory), you ought to think more about it now....

Consider an eager-beaver novice with his/her first fixed disk:

Counting on an endless amount of disk space, the novice copies all of the information on his/her removable disks onto the fixed disk. The files in the root directories of the removable disks go into the root directory of the fixed disk. Maybe the novice uses a few directories—but almost all of these grow out of the root.

The result of all this haste? The fixed disk quickly fills up with garbage. The listing for the root directory looks like a phone book. Files of the same names *overwrite* each other. Application programs thus crash, because not all their files are available.

Messes like this are seldom really straightened out. The novice's more knowledgeable friends can't help—because it's almost beyond hope—and the novice won't erase the files and start over because it took so much time copying them there in the first place. He/she finds a handful of programs that do work and leaves the rest of the fixed disk as a wasteland.

Challenge: Avoid the novice's mistakes.

Solutions: When you get a new fixed disk, install a single applications program—one that you actually need to use—and make sure it works. Then, when you need another program, install *it* (only) and test it.

Do not install a program on the fixed disk until you need to use it. Do not transfer data to a fixed disk until you need to access that data.

Keep your root clean. Only five *files* should be in the root directory:

    IO.SYS
    MSDOS.SYS
    COMMAND.COM
    CONFIG.SYS
    AUTOEXEC.BAT

The rest of the items in the root directory should be *other directories.**

Do not grow all directories from the root—group related directories together. For example, instead of having the directories of several game programs grow from the root, create one **\GAMES** directory. Then put all the *directories* of games into **\GAMES**.

---

*A few programs are naughty and insist on putting files into the root directory. In those cases, you just can't help it.

Investigating Unknown Computer Systems

After you get your own customizing and disk strategy under control, you're ready to start trying to understand other people's DOS computers. Yep—that's right—you've reached the point in this course where you can start *helping other people*.

So imagine that you're trying to help your friend with his DOS computer (he/she's having lots of trouble, you see). You sit down at his computer and suddenly realize that you know nothing about his/her system, its organization, it contents—nothing. What do you do?

You methodically work through this **investigation checklist**:

a.   Find the DOS prompt. An applications program might be running. If so, exit the program, or—if all else fails—try rebooting the computer; maybe you'll at least get back to a Shell menu, if not the prompt itself.

b.   Enter **VER** to find out what version of DOS you have here. If it's a recent version, such as 5.0, you know that almost all of the DOS commands are at your disposal. But an older version, such as 2.1, will have fewer commands.

c. Enter A:, B:, C:, etc., until you get this error: **Invalid disk drives: drive specification**. This tells you how many disk drives are in the system. For the remainder of this example, suppose there's just one fixed disk (the C: drive) and one floppy disk drive (the A: drive).

d. Enter C: to make that the default drive. Enter **CD** to see what directory is the default directory at the moment. Then enter **CD ** to move to the root directory (make it the default). Enter **DIR /p** to get a first browsing look at your friend's disk structure.

e. Find the directory containing the external DOS commands. Hopefully, this will be named something like **\DOS** (try **DIR \DOS** to see if this is the case). But don't be surprised if all of the external DOS commands are in the root directory.

f. If you still can't find the commands yet, enter **PATH** to see what paths have been set. It's quite possible that no paths are set. However, this could be a clue as to the location of the DOS commands. If you get a list of paths, run a directory of each one to see if that's where the DOS commands are.

g.   Once you've found the DOS commands, you must make the external commands available to you for further exploration:

- If the DOS commands are in the root directory, they're available to you now.

- If the current **PATH** leads to the commands, they're available to you now.

- If **PATH** is not used, enter **PATH C:**name, where name is the directory where you found the DOS commands.

- If none of the above works, ask your friend for his/her DOS disks. Make **A:** the default drive, and access the commands through your friend's removable disks.

- If *that* doesn't work, get your own DOS working disks and reboot the computer with them. Make **A:** the default, and access the commands through your own removable DOS working disks.

h.   Now that you have the powerful external commands to call upon, get a handle on the disk tree: Try **TREE C:** or **TREE C:\ | MORE** or **TREE C:\ >PRN** so that you can study the tree structure at your leisure.

Notice if the tree is flat (all directories growing out of the root)—a sign of user inexperience. By contrast, a bushy ("well-branched") tree tells you that he/she has put some thought into the disk's organization. Look for directories of common programs, such as **123** or **WP**.

i. Run a **CHKDSK C:\ /F**, to see if your friend's disk has any lost clusters. A disk with a lot of lost clusters indicates an inexperienced user—he/she probably reboots the computer frequently from within programs, thus messing up the File Allocation Table (**FAT**).

j. If you're merely curious about the disk, skip this step. But if you really want to help your friend solve problems, run **CHKDSK** to get a complete list of the files and directories.

You could enter **CHKDSK C: /V > PRN**, to print out a copy on your friend's printer (time consuming and maybe not too slick); or you could put one of your own removable disks into the **A:** drive and enter **CHKDSK C: /V > A:\VERBOSE.TXT**. This puts the verbose listing into a text file that you can study later—from your own system.

k. Examine the **CONFIG.SYS** and **AUTOEXEC.BAT** files, if any, to see how the computer is customized. Make sure they're in the root directory!

If you've worked through this list, then chances are, you're going to discover the problems your friend has been having (maybe it's just understanding on his/her part—in which case, why not offer him/her this book?).

Do You Have It Together?

1. Do the **CONFIG.SYS** and **AUTOEXEC.BAT** files come on your DOS disks? What are the differences between these two files? If you enter their names (as keywords), will either file run?

2. In the **CONFIG.SYS** file, what if you reverse the order of these two settings?   **FILES=20**   **BREAK=ON**

    In the **AUTOEXEC.BAT** file, what if you reverse the order of these two commands?   **DOSSHELL   MOUSE > NUL**

3. With **BREAK=OFF** in **CONFIG.SYS**, will `CTRL` `BREAK` stop programs?

4. Can you start *WordPerfect* by booting your computer?

5. If you start copying all your removable disks to the root directory of your new fixed disk, what will happen? Are there some files which you should never copy to a fixed disk?

6. Your family has a new computer with a big 160-Mb fixed disk. Hundreds of games have been copied to the fixed disk, but many don't work. Your mission: Study the system and fix things.

Totally Together

1. **CONFIG.SYS** and **AUTOEXEC.BAT** do not come on your DOS disks. If your version of *DOS* has an install disk, these two files will be made for you during the installation process. Otherwise, you have to make them yourself.

   CONFIG.SYS specifies certain internal *DOS* settings that CONFIGure the computer SYStem. **AUTOEXEC.BAT** is a batch file which is executed automatically whenever the computer is booted.

   CONFIG.SYS is not a program you can run by giving its name as a keyword command. It is examined by DOS during the boot process. Yes, **AUTOEXEC** is the keyword to run **AUTOEXEC.BAT**, which is a batch file. Also, *DOS* runs **AUTOEXEC.BAT** when the computer is booted. However, running **AUTOEXEC** manually is usually *not a good idea* because some utilities may be installed into memory more than once, creating the potential for bugs.

2. The order of the settings in a **CONFIG.SYS** file doesn't matter—nor do all of the settings need to be present. The order of items in an **AUTOEXEC.BAT** file *does* matter—the commands and keywords are executed from top to bottom. So if **DOSSHELL** were listed before **MOUSE**, the DOS Shell would start before the mouse program was installed—the Shell would be launched, but your mouse wouldn't work.

3. **BREAK=OFF** means that DOS will checks for CTRL BREAK—but only when the program is expecting keyboard input (capable programmers, though, can make their programs totally ignore CTRL BREAK).

4. You can automatically start *WordPerfect* (or any other program) at boot time. At the very end of your **AUTOEXEC.BAT** file, insert:

    ```
    C:
    CD \WP        (change to the directory with the program)
    WP            (give the keyword of the program)
    CD \
    ```

5. If you just dump everything indiscriminately into the root directory of your fixed disk, files of the same names will overwrite each other, causing an unworkable mess.

    You shouldn't copy old projects (which you'll never need again) onto your hard disk.

6. First, explore this unknown computer:

a. The computer has a strange looking menu system. But one of the menu items is **Command line prompt**. You select this item and find yourself at the DOS prompt.

b. Enter **VER** and find out that DOS version 4.01 is installed. So, all of the DOS commands are accessible via this version.

c. You can see the **A:** and **B:** drives, but you test them with **A:** and **B:**. Then you enter **C:** to verify that there is, in fact, the fixed disk (there'd better be, after all the money you paid for it!). Finally, you enter **D:** and get an error message—no more disk drives are present.

d. You enter **C:**, then **CD**, and note the current default directory. Then **CD ** and **DIR /p** and browse your way through gobs of files and directories on the screen. This gives you your first clue that the disk is organized poorly.

e. Since this a new computer, DOS is probably installed with an *Install* disk. On that hunch, you enter **DIR \DOS** and sure enough—there are the DOS commands.

f. You enter **PATH** and see that **C:\DOS** is a path. More good luck: You can use all the DOS commands as though they were internal.

g. Since the DOS commands are in a directory which is included in the **PATH** command, you don't have to do anything further to make them accessible to you.

h. You enter **TREE > PRN** to print out a copy of the tree structure (to come back and study later).

i. You enter **CHKDSK /F** and see that the disk has some lost clusters.

j. Enter **CHKDSK /V ! SORT > PRN** to send an alphabetized list of all files and directories to the printer (for later study).

k. Enter **PRINT CONFIG.SYS** and **PRINT AUTOEXEC.BAT** so that you can study these important files later.

Now study the printouts from the above steps to get a layout of the disk. You can probably save many of the programs and files:

• Make a **\GAMES** directory. With this many game programs, you should probably subdivide **\GAMES** even further (for example, **\GAMES\BOARD** and **\GAMES\CARD**).

• *Test* each game program. *If it works,* copy it to the **\GAMES** directory, then erase the original. Erase the games that don't work, so they don't take up valuable space on the fixed disk.

• Put any non-game programs into their appropriate directories. When finished, you should have a well-organized disk tree with only the five bootup files in the root directory (**IO.SYS, MSDOS.SYS, COMMAND.COM, CONFIG.SYS**, and **AUTOEXEC.BAT**).

• Teach your family how to access the **\GAMES** directory.

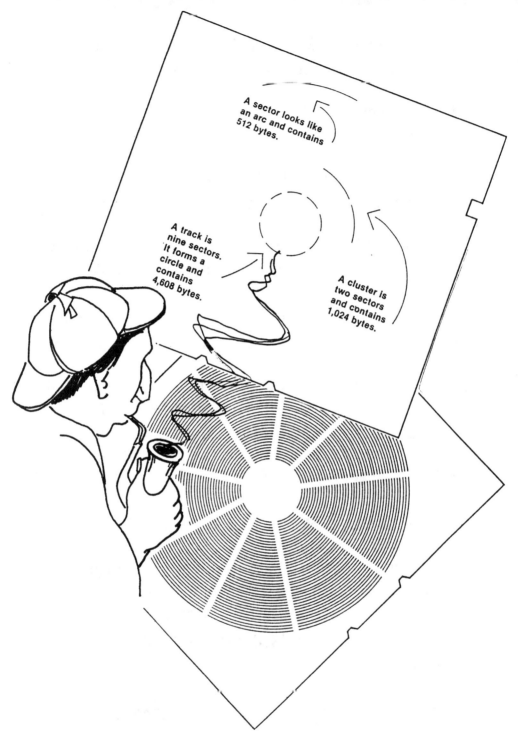

A sector looks like an arc and contains 512 bytes.

A track is nine sectors. It forms a circle and contains 4,608 bytes.

A cluster is two sectors and contains 1,024 bytes.

14. BEHIND THE SCENES

"Bytes and Files and Hex—Oh, My!"

Get out your magnifying glass—you're going to do some investigative work now. Of course, if you're *really* not interested in this technical stuff, you can skip this chapter. But don't. This is easy and *fascinating*. You'll get a much better "feel" for how a computer really works: You're going to examine DOS files in detail, find "missing" bytes on disks, look inside the **CPU** and your computer's memory, etc.—all that kind of behind-the-scenes stuff. And first, you'll learn about hex....

Hex is not a witch's spell (though it might seem just about as cryptic). "Hex" is short for "hexadecimal numerical system," and it's important because DOS displays files and other information in that numbering system. A hexadecimal numbering system is based on the value 16, using the digits **0 - 9** and **A - F** (a total of 16 digits).

By now you know about bytes (a collection of 8 bits). And half a byte (4 bits) is a *nibble*. So here's how to count in decimal, nibble, and hex:

Decimal	=	Nibble	=	**Hex**	Decimal	=	Nibble	=	**Hex**
0	=	0000	=	**0**	8	=	1000	=	**8**
1	=	0001	=	**1**	9	=	1001	=	**9**
2	=	0010	=	**2**	10	=	1010	=	**A**
3	=	0011	=	**3**	11	=	1011	=	**B**
4	=	0100	=	**4**	12	=	1100	=	**C**
5	=	0101	=	**5**	13	=	1101	=	**D**
6	=	0110	=	**6**	14	=	1110	=	**E**
7	=	0111	=	**7**	15	=	1111	=	**F**

Thus, for example, decimal 12 = nibble 1100 = hex C

As you can see, nibbles come in exactly 16 variations—and hex numbers have exactly 16 possible characters, so *one hex digit can represent one nibble.*

Therefore, since a byte contains exactly *two* nibbles, *any byte can be represented by exactly two hex digits.* The first hex digit corresponds to the first nibble of the byte; the second hex digit represents the second nibble of the byte:

Since	nibble 0001		=	hex **1**	
and		nibble 1111	=		hex **F**
therefore	byte 0001 1111		=	hex **1F**	

So *hex is a very concise way of displaying bytes.* Each byte can be displayed as 2 hex digits rather than 8 bits (binary digits—0's and 1's), so *four times as many bytes can be displayed in the same number of printed or displayed characters.*

That's all you have to know about hex for normal DOS applications: It exists, it uses the characters **A** through **F** as additional numerals, and it's a convenient way to compactly represent the values of nibbles and bytes.

Using the DEBUG Program

DEBUG is a special "programmer's program" provided with DOS. It lets you view the inner structure—the bytes—of program files. Similar to **EDLIN**, **DEBUG** has its own prompt (-) and commands.

As a good first example, try using **DEBUG** to see inside a simple _text_ file (if you have no fixed disk, copy **DEBUG** to your _Power_ disk)....

Hm: Use **DEBUG** to view the file **A:\WORD\PEOPLE\SHOP.TXT**.

Go: With the _Power_ disk in the **A:** drive, enter this:
          TYPE A:\WORD\PEOPLE\SHOP.TXT

That's what the file normally looks like to you—text, right?. But now enter **DEBUG A:\WORD\PEOPLE\SHOP.TXT**

Now the **DEBUG** command loads the file into memory (you should see the **DEBUG** hyphen prompt). So enter **D** (for **D**ump) and **DEBUG** dumps the contents of **SHOP.TXT** to the screen.

Down the _left side_ of the dump are hex numbers—something like **7647:0100** (your numbers are probably different). These numbers show the **address** of the file—its location in the computer's memory.

In the _middle_ of the screen is the **_hex dump_** of the file itself (remember: each two-digit hex number represents a byte). The hyphens down the middle are simply formatting for your eyes—to separate the first eight bytes in a line from the second eight bytes.

Down the *right side* of the screen is the same **SHOP.TXT** file listed in **alphabetical** characters (non-alphabet characters appear as **.**).

Look closely at the hex dump: Each letter of the alphabet in **SHOP.TXT** is represented in the hex dump by its **ASCII** code—just a simple substitution. For example, the first item the text file is the word **Milk**:

hex	**4D**	**69**	**6C**	**6B**
bits	0100 1101	0110 1001	0110 1100	0110 1011
ASCII decimal value	77	105	108	107
ASCII characters	**M**	**i**	**l**	**k**

Then you see is **0D 0A**—so translate them:

hex **0D** = 00001101 = decimal 13 = **Carriage Return (CR)**
hex **0A** = 00001010 = decimal 10 = **Line Feed (LF)**

Carriage Return and Line Feed are the results of your pressing ←ENTER *on the keyboard* (think about it: the cursor returns to the left edge *and* advances a line)!

Continuing you see, **45 67 67 73**, the hex code for **Eggs**—once again, followed by **0D 0A**, or ←ENTER. Likewise, **48 61 6D** stands for "**Ham**". (and then you pressed **0D 0A** again).

The last byte in the file* is the second byte on the second line: **1A**. This is none other than your old friend, the caboose byte:

hex **1A** = 00011010 = decimal 26 = **^Z**

which is what you knew you were getting by pressing F6 or CTRL-Z!

---

*The other bytes in the dump don't mean anything. They're still the hex characters that previously occupied that memory address and will remain until some file overwrites that part of the memory.

Using the DOS Shell to View Hex Dumps

Well, that's a good first peek at the individual bytes in a file. Now **Q**uit **DEBUG** by entering **Q** and you'll return to the _DOS_ prompt.

Frankly, **DEBUG** is difficult to use. You have to deal with yet another prompt (the hyphen) and a whole new set of commands. But with DOS version 4.00 or later, the DOS Shell makes hex dumps _easier to view_ (if you don't have the Shell installed on a fixed disk, skip this page)....

Challenge: Use the DOS Shell to view the hex display of **SHOP.TXT**.

Solution: So easy, it's embarrassing:

Enter **DOSSHELL** to start the Shell.
Select **File System** to enter the File System.
Select **A**, to display the files in the **A:** drive.
Select **\WORD\PEOPLE**, to display the files in that directory, then **SHOP.TXT**, the file of interest.
Select **File** and **View**, to display **SHOP.TXT**.
At the bottom of the screen, select **Hex/ASCII**
...and there it is!

You'll notice one big difference between this display and the **DEBUG** display: The caboose byte and all the meaningless bytes after it _are not displayed_.

Press ⌜ESC⌝, ⌜F3⌝, and ⌜F3⌝ again to exit the DOS Shell. All right, now you know how to _view_ bytes. But how well can you _count_ bytes?...

Do This: **FORMAT** your *Power Backup* disk* and leave it in the **A:** drive. The display should indicate a total disk space of **362,496** bytes.** Hmmm... something's missing here— about 6,144 bytes! A 360K disk has 360 x 1,024 = 368,640 bytes—but your display shows that only 362,496 bytes are available. That's 6,144 short!

Quest: Find those missing bytes.

Clue: *6,144 bytes is an even 6 kilobytes.* That is, 6 x 1,024 = 6,144. Coincidence? Nope: Since a *cluster* is equal to 1K in this size disk, this means that exactly six clusters are "missing in action." And *here's what happened to those six clusters* when you formatted the disk:

> 1 cluster was allocated (reserved) for the *boot record;*
> 2 were allocated for the **F**ile **A**llocation **T**able (**FAT**).
> 3 were allocated for the *root directory.*

So DOS takes 6K of your disk and doesn't even tell you about it. A newly-formatted disk isn't totally blank.

So, the first part of the mystery is solved—but you're not finished....

* It's OK to destroy your backup for a moment for this demonstration—just be sure to make a fresh backup of your *Power* disk when you're finished.

**Note: These examples are for DOS version 4.01 and a 360K removable disk. However, the same principals apply to other versions of DOS—and other sizes of disks.

The Mystery of the Missing Bytes, Part 2

Do This: Copy your DOS **COMMAND.COM** file to your newly-formatted *Power Backup* disk. Then enter **DIR A:**. You'll see that the **COMMAND.COM** file is **37,557** bytes long and that **324,608** bytes are left available on the disk....

"Uh... hmmm... if the disk had 362,496 bytes before—and then **COMMAND.COM** used 37,557 of them—that *should* leave 324,939 bytes now. But the **DIR**ectory listing says that only 324,608 bytes are left—that's 331 bytes off!" (Yep.)

Sigh: Figure out what DOS did with those 331 bytes.

Aha: Remember how **DEBUG** displayed those extra "meaningless" bytes after the **SHOP.TXT** file? It did so because *DOS stores and retrieves files from disks in clusters.*

So when **COMMAND.COM** was copied to the disk, it required 37 *full clusters* (37,888 bytes), even though it was actually only 37,557 bytes long. The **DIR**ectory listing tells you the actual size of the file itself (**37,557**), but when calculating the memory still available, it knows that the rest of that 37th cluster is not available; generally, DOS doesn't put parts of two different files into the same cluster. It counts exactly but "keeps the change."

Now, you needed to know *that* in order to learn the next fundamental principle of DOS files—how DOS *finds* them in the first place....

As you know, a file is a "byte train," and it has a caboose—an *end* byte (^Z), which you saw with **DEBUG** a few pages ago. *But there's no special byte that means "this is the <u>start</u> of the file."* So how does DOS find the beginning of a file? That depends on where the file is....

Finding Files on Disks

On disks, the process is quite straightforward: The disk directory contains the name of the file, and the **F**ile **A**llocation **T**able (**FAT**) contains—in sequential order—the numbers of the clusters where the file is stored. Since (as you just read), DOS generally writes a new file beginning with a new cluster, when DOS needs to read that file again, it simply starts reading at the file's *first* cluster. If the end of a file falls somewhere in the middle of a cluster, the remaining bytes are read but ignored—wasted, as you just saw.

Finding Files in RAM

A computer's internal memory (RAM) doesn't have sectors or clusters, so the disk method of finding the beginning of a file doesn't work for a file in RAM. Instead, the computer uses an address system.

Every byte in the computer's memory has an ***address***, consisting of two 4-digit hex numbers (in other words, it's two *2-byte* numbers, or two *16-bit* numbers), separated for readability by a colon—as in the **DEBUG** display you saw earlier.

Take an example—here's an address: **10AF:C3D2**

The first half of this address is like the "street number"—called the *segment*. The second half is the "house number"—called the *offset*.

$$\textbf{10AF} = \text{"street number"} = segment$$
$$\textbf{C3D2} = \text{"house number"} = offset$$

This is the general pattern that DOS uses to address RAM

There are some variations, too: Sometimes if a programmer is doing a lot of work "on the same street," then he/she can omit the segment part of an address. For example, **C3D2** might be given as an address, if it's clear that he/she is working on "street" **10AF**.

Also DOS sometimes shows addresses in a "rural route" system. The first byte's address is simply "Box 1," and the numbers progress all the way to the end of (RAM). This system uses six hex digits (e.g. **01CEC2**). You saw an example of this addressing scheme in the left column of the DOS Shell hex display earlier in this chapter.

But no matter how it's represented, one fact remains: *Every byte in a computer's memory has its own address.*

Therefore, to find the start of a file, DOS must simply find the address of the *first* byte in the file. Then all of the remaining bytes in the file are just "down the street." And how does DOS find this address? It's the "postmaster!" When the computer is booted and DOS initializes itself, it reserves a portion of RAM to keep track of things—the DOS "Post Office," if you will—a list of who's who on the route and what their addresses are.

To get a glimpse of what the "DOS Post Office" looks like, you need another command—the **MEM** (**MEM**ory) command—available in DOS versions 4.00 and later.

Do It: **MEM** is an external command; if you don't have a fixed disk, find it on the *Working 2* disk. When it's available, enter **MEM**.

So? By itself, **MEM** displays how much memory your computer has and how much is available (shrug).

But: Enter **MEM /PROGRAM**

Ah: You should see something like this:

```
Address    Name       Size    Type
-------    -------    ------  ---------
000700     IO         0020D0  System Program
0027D0     MSDOS      008E20  System Program
```

It's a list of everything currently in your computer's memory (only the lines for **IO.SYS** and **MSDOS.SYS** are shown above). **IO.SYS** is located at the (hex) **000700** address and is (hex) **20D0**, or (decimal) 8,400 bytes long.

The point here is this: When DOS loads a program into memory, *the program's address is stored in this list.* Then, when DOS wants to know where a program begins in memory, it just looks up the address at this "Post Office."

Memory Types

While personal computer memory has grown to "big city" size, the "post office" has remained "small town." Because of the limitations of the original IBM PC, personal computer memory has had a 640K barrier. There are now ways to "break the barrier," but to do so, you need to know about the types of personal computer memory.

A computer's memory is stored on a series of memory chips, called a memory bank—like a "tape measure" of memory:

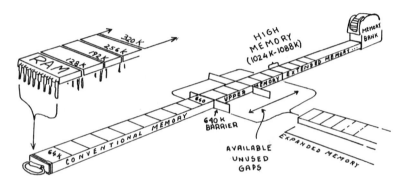

The first chip in the tape measure starts at zero memory and each additional chip adds a chunk of additional memory. The first 640K of memory is Conventional Memory—where programs ran on the original IBM PC. More memory was present (up to 1,024K) but was set aside for special uses, such as helping with video displays. This is called Upper Memory, because it's "above" the Conventional Memory.

As programs grew and pushed against the 640K limit, the pros tried to squeeze more memory into play. Upper Memory had some unused gaps, so they developed Expanded Memory to squeeze into those gaps. But not all of the Expanded Memory could fit at once into the gaps; it had to be "shuffled" in and out—a slow and not-ideal solution.

Happily, as chip technology has improved, memory has been *extended* "straight out," more logically, all positioned "higher" than the 1,024K marker. The first 64K of Extended Memory is called High Memory.

Here's a summary of the various memory types:

Type	Address
Conventional	0K - 640K
Upper	640K - 1,024K
Expanded	(Squeezed into Upper)
High	1,024K - 1,088K
Extended	Greater than 1,024K

DOS 5 helps you take advantage of these different types of memory. Three new features in particular* are items to be included early in the **CONFIG.SYS** file—before any other **DEVICE** entries.**

```
DEVICE=C:\DOS\HIMEM.SYS
DOS=HIGH,UMB
DEVICE=C:\DOS\EMM386.EXE 512 RAM
```

HIMEM stands for **HI**gh **MEM**ory and manages both High Memory and Extended Memory. **UMB** stands for **U**pper **M**emory **B**lock. It tells DOS to install itself in High Memory and use Upper Memory. **EMM386** stands for **E**xpanded **M**emory e**M**ulator for **386**, which uses Extended Memory as a substitute for Expanded Memory. Specifically, the item **512 RAM** tells DOS to use 512K of Extended Memory RAM to *emulate* Expanded Memory. Thus, programs that were designed for use with Expanded Memory can work with Extended Memory instead.

*DOS 5 has other memory tricks for adventuresome souls. See your DOS manual for details.

**These assume that you have a 386 CPU or better, with Extended but no Expanded Memory.

Inside Your CPU

To *really* understand bytes and their roles as carriers of data and instructions in your DOS computer, you can't just look at them as they sit in files. You must follow them as they enter the master control center of your computer—the **C**entral **P**rocessing **U**nit (**CPU**).

Imagine the **CPU** as an old rolltop desk with lots of cubbyholes. The computer (via instructions from the programmer) takes things out of the cubbyholes and places them "on the desk" to be worked on. *Registers*, which have specific names and uses, do the work. The CPU loads these registers, changes the values in them, if appropriate, and sends the results back out to memory.

Ready? Use **DEBUG** to display your computer's CPU registers.

Watch: Enter **DEBUG** (no file name), and you'll see its - prompt. Then enter **R**, for **R**egisters and see something like this:

```
AX=0000 BX=0000 CX=002D DX=0000 SP=FFEE BP=0000
SI=0000 DI=0000 DS=76EE ES=76EE SS=76EE CS=76EE
IP=0100 NV UP EI PL NZ NA PO NC
76EE:0100 FEC2 INC DL DS:0000=CD
```

This is a list of the CPU registers, showing the name of each register and the (hex) value currently stored in it.

Look at this listing in more detail....

First, the *general purpose registers:*

$$AX=0000 \quad BX=0000 \quad CX=002D \quad DX=0000$$

The names of these general registers are **AX**, **BX**, **CX**, and **DX**. A programmer can put values into them and do calculations there. Each register can hold a two-byte (16-bit) value—represented here by four hex digits. In the above example, **AX**, **BX**, and **DX** are each holding the (hex) value **0000** (zero) right now; **CX** happens to have the hex value **002D** (these values are random at this point; they might be anything).

Each of these general purpose registers, in turn, is made of two other one-byte registers—the High byte and the Low byte:

AH AL **BH BL** **CH CL** **DH DL**

AH = **A** High

AL = **A** Low

Thus, **AH** linked with **AL** becomes **AX**, etc.

Those are the general purpose registers. Other registers have *specific* purposes:

SP is the "Stack Pointer" register. "Pointer" is just another word for "address," so the Stack Pointer contains the *address* of the **stack**, which is like a corner of a desk where you might stack stuff you're going to need soon, but not right now. The value—in this case **FFEE**—is the address that tells the CPU where to find the stack.

BP is the Base Pointer register. It holds an address that the CPU uses to track values within the stack.

SI is the **S**ource **I**ndex register.

DI is the **D**estination **I**ndex register. If you're copying a file, you're taking each byte in turn from one file and putting it into another file. The Source Index register contains the *address* of the first file; the Destination Index register the *address* of the second file.

DS is the **D**ata **S**egment register. It contains the current "street number" where the data for a program is being kept in memory.

ES is the **E**xtra **S**egment register—for sophisticated programming.

SS is the **S**tack **S**egment register, which contains the "street number" of the stack's address. This value combines with that of the Stack Pointer (**SP**) to form the address of a particular byte in the stack: **SS:SP**

CS is the **C**ode **S**egment register.

IP is the **I**nstruction **P**ointer register. The values in **CS** and **IP** combine (**CS:IP**) to form the address of the instruction byte which the computer is currently reading.

One register is a collection of *flags*: **NV UP EI PL NZ NA PO NC** Each two-letter name here represents an individual *bit* (not a byte, a *bit*), called a *flag*, which can be either off or on (down or up). The **CPU** uses these flags (and a programmer manipulates them) to determine the status of various CPU processes.

For example, the second flag is shown as being **UP** (the alternative being **DN**, for **D**ow**N**). This is the *direction* flag, used in handling data: When the computer reads data, it checks the status of this flag: It reads data in a forward direction when this flag is **UP**; backwards if it's **DN**.

The last line of the CPU register display is the ***status line***, which tells you exactly where you are—and what's happening—in the current program. The information in this line is what programmers use for debugging (fixing errors). That's why **DEBUG** is named as it is.

Take a closer look:

76EE:0100   is the *address* of the next instruction to be performed by the computer. In other words, it's the address formed by the values in registers **CS : IP**.

FEC2   is *the next instruction*. Since you've not written a program yet, this code is just random garbage— whatever happened to be left there from the previous program.

INC DL   is the *assembly-language name* for the next instruction value **FEC2**. **INC** stands for **INC**rement; **INC DL** means to "increment the value in the **DL** register."

DS:0000=CD   is the *address* (**DS : 0000**) and *value* (**CD**) of the next *data* byte.

So that's a short tour of the CPU registers. As you can see, *most of computing at this level is a matter of bookkeeping:* Where is the file of instructions to run? What's the next instruction? Where is it? What's the data it's supposed to work on? Where's *that?* And so on.

Enter **Q** now to get out of **DEBUG** and return to the DOS prompt.

Interrupts

Programs often are constructed using special "prepackaged" modules, called subroutines, that accomplish specific tasks—usually common, repetitive ones. An ***interrupt*** is the technical name for a special kind of subroutine*—a subroutine that *interrupts* your program to do something else.

In addition to everything else you've seen DOS do, it also provides over 100 interrupts—to do things such as display characters, end programs, etc.

The **MEM**ory command can show you where the interrupts are located.

Do It: Enter **MEM /PROGRAM** and notice the line that looks like this

Address	Name	Size	Type
000000		000400	Interrupt Vector

This shows that the interrupts are the very first things in memory, at address **000000**, and that they are hex 400 bytes long.

---

*Why did they call it "interrupt" instead of "subroutine?" Because of the **MINI** Rule: They **M**ade **I**t, so they got to **N**ame **I**t.

In assembly-level programming code, you invoke an interrupt (call this special kind of subroutine) with an **INT** command. Here are two important interrupt (**INT**) commands:

INT 20   This is the last instruction in most programs (kind of a "caboose" for programs). **INT 20** terminates your program and returns control back to DOS. If you write an assembly language program and forget to end it, the program will keep right on running—trying to "obey" the extraneous bytes that immediately follow your program in memory. The industry catch phrase for this is "unpredictable results will occur" (the keyboard usually locks up and you have to reboot—sometimes data is lost also).*

INT 21   **INT 21** *is actually many interrupts in one. What it does depends on the value in the* **AH** *register.* For example, with a value of **02** in **AH**, **INT 21** displays a character on the screen. The character it displays depends on the value in the **DL** register.

You'll get to practice with **INT 20** and **INT 21** in just a few pages. As for the other interrupts, you can read more about them—if you wish—in programming manuals.

---

*This is called the "crash test," in comparison with making an airplane: You make it and push it over the cliff. After it crashes, you fix it and try again until it *doesn't* crash! An amazing number of computer programs are written this way.

An Assembly-Level Program

You've read throughout this Easy Course about the **ASCII** code. You know that certain characters are represented by certain bytes, and you've seen examples for particular characters here and there. But you've never seen a list.

The Last Hurrah: Write an *assembly-language* program to display the **ASCII** characters valued from decimal 32 to decimal 127*—that's hex **20** to hex **7F**.

Hurrah: Put the *Power* disk into the **A:** drive.
Make an **\ASSEMBLY** directory to store your program (**MD \ASSEMBLY**).
Make this the default (**CD \ASSEMBLY**).
Enter **A:\DOS\DEBUG** to load the debugger and see its - prompt.

(*cont.* --->)

---

*The characters valued below decimal 32 do special things—Line Feed and Carriage Return, etc.— so they'll interfere with a display. The characters valued above decimal 127 *vary* in different computing devices—mainly some non-IBM printers. For example, if you have **ASCII** characters over decimal 127 on your video screen (which happens to include all of those neat little lines that form boxes and windows) and you press **PRINT SCREEN** with one of these offbeat printers, you'll get *italic* alphabetic characters *instead of lines and boxes*.

Enter **A** to start the **Assembly**.

You'll see some address, such as **342B:0100**. The **342B** is the code segment—the "street address" of the program in memory (your machine probably has a different value for this code segment). Then the **0100** is the address in this segment (the "house number") where the program actually begins; **DEBUG** assembly language programs start at address **0100**.

Now enter, line by line, the following program instructions (after each line, the next address will be displayed by **DEBUG**):

MOV DL,20 moves the value hex **20** into the **DL** register. Hex **20** (decimal 32) is the **ASCII** value of the first character to be displayed.

MOV CX,0060 moves the value hex **0060** into the **CX** register. This program will have a loop that repeats for each of the **ASCII** characters being listed. The **CX** register will count down —from a value you name—to zero as the program loops. As long as **CX** is greater than zero, the program keeps on looping. You want to list 96—that's hex **0060**— characters.

MOV AH,02 moves the value hex **02** into the **AH** register. This tells DOS that if it encounters an **INT 21**, it should display a character (recall page 310).

INT 21   (here it is) displays the character whose value is currently stored in the **DL** register.

INC DL   *increments* (i.e. increases by one) the value in **DL** to the next **ASCII** character value.

LOOP 0107   **LOOP**s back to address **0107** (where the **INT 21** instruction is) *if* the value in register **CX** is greater than zero. If **CX = 0000**, then the **LOOP** is *ignored*; the next instruction is performed.

INT 20   Ends the program and returns control to DOS.

After the last line, just press (←ENTER) and **DEBUG** will go back to the hyphen prompt.

Try It Out: Enter **G** for Go and you should see something like:

```
!"#$%&'()*+,.0123456789:;<=>?@ABCDEF
GHIJKLMNOPQRSTUVWXYZ[\]^_`abcdefghijk
lmnopqrstuvwxyz{|}~
```

Sure enough—a display of **ASCII** text characters in sequence! (The first character—to the left of the exclamation point—is the space character.)

Now Snoop: You should now be back at **DEBUG**'s – prompt. To get a better look at the program, you can enter **U** for Unassemble. You'll see something like:

```
342B:0100   B220     MOV DL,20
342B:0102   B96000   MOV CX,0060
342B:0105   B402     MOV AH,02
342B:0107   CD21     INT 21
342B:0109   FEC2     INC DL
342B:010B   E2FA     LOOP 0107
342B:010D   CD20     INT 20
```

(plus several lines of garbage)

This is similar to what you've seen before, except a new column has appeared in the middle. This middle column displays the actual byte values (in hex) of each instruction *in machine code.* For example, **B220** is the two bytes in machine code that accomplish **MOV DL,20**.

You can see that all of the machine-level instructions in the example are two bytes long, except the second one, **B96000**, which is three bytes long; this program is 15 bytes long.

Also notice how the address pointer in the left column increases after each machine-level instruction by the number of bytes in that instruction.

Storing Your Program

Your first assembly-level program is now written and you want to save it to the *Power* disk. But how?

Like So: At the **DEBUG** prompt, enter **N SEEASCII.COM**. The **N** stands for **N**ame; the name you're giving to the program is **SEEASCII**. The **COM** extension in the file name means that this is a **COM**mand file—a program!

Next, you must tell **DEBUG** how long your program is. It's 15 bytes, which is **000F** in hex. You must put this value into registers **BX** and **CX**—half of the digits in each register. At the **DEBUG** prompt (-), enter **R BX** (for **R**egister **BX**), and you'll see the contents of the **BX** register. Enter the first two digits of the byte length: **00**. Then, for the other two digits, enter **R CX**, then **0F**.

You're now ready to write this program to the *Power* disk. Enter **W** (for **W**rite) at the - prompt, and it's done!

Enter **Q** for **Q**uit, to leave **DEBUG** and return to the DOS prompt. You can now run your new program without using **DEBUG**!

Just enter its keyword, **SEEASCII**, and presto—there it goes!

Final Exam

1.   The hex notation **B96000** represents how many bytes?

2.   What's a nibble?

3.   Why is hex notation convenient for programming?

4.   How is the **ASCII** code like a secret decoder ring?

5.   With the *Power* disk in the **A:** drive, view the **TODO.TXT** file with **DEBUG**: Enter **A:\DOS\DEBUG \WORD\PEOPLE\TODO.TXT** to load the file, and then **D** to get the hex dump. In the middle of the display, you should see these bytes:

31 2E 20 20 54 61 6B 65-20 6F 75 74 20 74 68 65

   a. What do they mean?

   b. Why is there a hyphen in the middle?

   c. What are the numbers down the left side of the screen?

   d. The display on the right side of the screen is for the actual characters in the file. Why are there so many periods?

6. View the hex dump of **TODO.TXT** with the DOS Shell. In what two ways is this display different from the **DEBUG** display?

7. In DOS version 4.01, **COMMAND.COM** is 37,557 bytes long, according to the **DIR**ectory. How many bytes does DOS use to store it on a disk?

8. Suppose you have *Sidekick*, a memory-resident program with a pop-up calculator and other features. You load *Sidekick* with your **AUTOEXEC.BAT** file and wonder if it's actually in memory. How can you look and see?

9. The following designations have to do with CPU registers and addresses. What do they mean?

CS:IP   SS:SP   SS:BP   DS:SI   ES:DI

10. What's the difference between an interrupt and a subroutine?

11. Once you've written a program with **DEBUG** and saved it to a disk, do you have to run **DEBUG** again to execute the program?

Blaze of Glory

1. Since two hex digits represent one byte, six hex digits would represent three bytes:

First byte	=	**B9**
Second byte	=	**60**
Third byte	=	**00**

2. A nibble is half a byte—four bits.

3. Hex is a convenient notation for programming because a nibble has exactly 16 variations and hex has exactly 16 characters—they match perfectly.

4. Both use simple substitution codes.

    For example, **A** = hex **41**. So whenever you see an **A**, you can read this as "hex **41**"—and vice versa.

5. The numbers in the middle of the screen are the hex digits for the bytes in the file. These are the code values—in hex notation—for **ASCII** characters

    a. Here's the one-to-one correspondence—note that hex **20** is the space character (**ASCII** decimal value, 32):

```
1  .        T  a  k  e     o  u  t     t  h  e
31 2E 20 20 54 61 6B 65-20 6F 75 74 20 74 68 65
```

    b. The hyphen in the middle is simply screen formatting—to help you visually separate the first eight bytes in the line from the second eight.

    c. The numbers down the left side of the screen are the addresses of the memory locations of the bytes in the file.

    d. Only alphabetic characters are displayed on the right side of the screen. All other bytes are displayed as periods.

(To get out of **DEBUG**, enter **Q** for **Quit**.)

6. Enter **DOSSHELL** and then select ...

```
File System
A
\WORD\PEOPLE TODO.TXT
File
View
HEX/ASCII
```

The DOS Shell hex dump and the **DEBUG** hex dump differ in the following two ways:

- The addresses are listed differently down the left sides of the displays. **DEBUG** uses the "street number/house number", or segment:offset, notation (such as **793B:0100**). The *DOS Shell* uses the "rural route" notation (such as **0794B0**).

- **DEBUG** displays the caboose byte and the succeeding "extra" bytes. The Shell's dump stops before the caboose byte.

Press (ESC), (F3), and (F3) again, to get back to the DOS prompt.

7. **COMMAND.COM** is 37,557 bytes long. To figure out how many clusters this is, divide 37,557 by 1,024 bytes/cluster(= 36.6768) and round *u*p (to 37). **COMMAND.COM**, therefore, uses 37 clusters of disk space, or (37 x 1,024 =) 37,888 bytes.

8. If you have version 4.00 or greater, the **MEM**ory command will show you if *Sidekick* is present. Enter **MEM /PROGRAM** to get a listing of what's in your computer's memory. If you see the keyword for *Sidekick* in this listing, then that program is in memory.

9. Each of the two-letter abbreviations denotes a register. Two registers together (separated by a colon) denote an address.

CS:IP (Code Segment:Instruction Pointer) The values in these registers indicate the memory address of the programming code currently being executed by the computer.

SS:SP (Stack Segment:Stack Pointer) The values in these registers indicate the memory address of a temporary stack of information.

SS:BP (Stack Segment:Base Pointer) The values in these registers indicate the memory address of a stack of information on a particular subroutine.

DS:SI (Data Segment:Source Index) The values in these registers indicate the memory address of the data that is about to be used.

ES:DI (Extra Segment:Destination Index) The values in these registers indicate the memory address where data will be put.

10. An interrupt is a special kind of subroutine, used to tell DOS to do some process (e.g. write a character). So all interrupts are subroutines, but not all subroutines are interrupts.

11. When you write a program with **DEBUG** and save it to a disk, the program then "stands on its own." You don't need **DEBUG** anymore; you can execute the program simply by entering its keyword (name).

15. Where to Go From Here

A book has a beginning and an end. But your learning and use of computers can go on and on. And DOS was well worth the time to learn, no? Now word processors, spreadsheets, databases, etc., let you do things that even huge mainframes couldn't do just a few years ago. What with desktop publishing, computer bulletin boards, education, etc., the computer revolution is just beginning—right in your home.

When you began this Easy Course, you may have been a bit intimidated by computers, mistakenly believing that they're intelligent—and that you'll never be smart enough to use them. Wrong. Computer "Artificial Intelligence" (**AI**) is just that—artificial. **AI** programs are written and stored in computers as bits and bytes—just like everything else in the computer. A computer running an **AI** program is still as dumb as a cinder block. The intelligence still comes from the humans that make and use computers. That's *you*!

So where do you go from here? You have your *Power* disk, but where's the power? It's in your knowledge and experience.

Some final tips: Whenever you want to make a change to your fixed disk, try it out first on a practice disk—such as your *Power* disk. Or, if you're using only removable disks, did you notice this course's habit of transferring DOS commands to the *Power* disk? When you have an actual project going on a removable disk, you can likewise copy the appropriate commands to that disk, so that they're readily available.

Also: Consult the DOS manuals. While it's true that their explanations can be downright confusing to many people, you now have a head start—a good idea what the commands can do. So explore the manuals confidently—to see what else you can learn!

APPENDICES

A: Commands and Versions

The version number for each command means that the command is included in that DOS version *and all later versions.*

APPEND	"APPEND"	External	DOS 3.2
ASSIGN	"ASSIGN"	External	PC 2.0 / MS 3.0
ATTRIB	"ATTRIBute"	External	DOS 3.0
BACKUP	"BACKUP"	External	DOS 2.0
BASIC	"BASIC"	External	PC 1.0
BASICA	"BASIC, Advanced"	External	PC 1.0
BREAK	"BREAK"	Internal	DOS 2.0
CHCP	"CHange Code Page"	Internal	DOS 3.3
CHDIR	"CHange DIRectory"	Internal	DOS 2.0
CD	"Change Directory"	Internal	DOS 2.0
CHKDSK	"CHecK DiSK"	External	DOS 1.0
CLS	"CLear Screen"	Internal	DOS 2.0
COMMAND	"Run COMMAND.COM"	External	DOS 1.0
COMP	"COMPare"	External	PC 1.0 / MS 3.3
COPY	"COPY"	Internal	DOS 1.0
CTTY	"Change TeleTYpe"	Internal	DOS 2.0
DATE	"DATE"	Internal	DOS 1.0
DEBUG	"DEBUG"	External	DOS 1.0
DEL	"DELete"	Internal	DOS 1.0
DELOLDOS	"DELete OLd DOS"	External	DOS 5.0
DIR	"DIRectory"	Internal	DOS 1.0
DISKCOMP	"DISK COMPare"	External	DOS 3.2
DISKCOPY	"DISK COPY"	External	DOS 2.0
DOSKEY	"DOS KEYboard"	External	DOS 5.0
DOSSHELL	"DOS SHELL"	External	DOS 4.0

EDIT	"EDITor"	External	DOS 5.0
EDLIN	"EDit LINe"	External	DOS 1.0
EMM386	"Expanded Memory eMulator for **386**"	External	DOS 5.0
ERASE	"ERASE"	External	DOS 1.0
EXE2BIN	"EXEcutable to **BIN**ary"	External	DOS 1.0
EXIT	"EXIT"	Internal	DOS 2.0
EXPAND	"EXPAND"	External	DOS 5.0
FASTOPEN	"FAST OPEN"	External	DOS 3.3
FC	"File Compare"	External	DOS 2.0
FIND	"FIND"	External	DOS 2.0
FDISK	"Fixed **DISK**"	External	DOS 3.2
FORMAT	"FORMAT"	External	DOS 1.0
GRAPHICS	"GRAPHICS"	External	DOS 2.0
GRAFTABL	"GRAph (F) **TABL**e"	External	DOS 3.0
GWBASIC	"Gee Whiz **BASIC**"	External	MS 1.0
HELP	"HELP"	External	DOS 5.0
JOIN	"JOIN"	External	DOS 3.0
KEYB	"KEYBoard"	External	DOS 3.2
LABEL	"LABEL"	External	DOS 3.1
LH	"Load High"	Internal	DOS 5.0
LINK	"LINK"	External	DOS 1.0
LOADFIX	"LOAD FIX"	External	DOS 5.0
LOADHIGH	"LOAD HIGH"	Internal	DOS 5.0
MD	"Make Directory"	Internal	DOS 2.0
MEM	"MEMory"	External	DOS 4.0
MIRROR	"MIRROR"	External	DOS 5.0
MKDIR	"MaKe DIRectory"	Internal	DOS 2.0
MODE	"MODE"	External	DOS 3.2
MORE	"MORE"	External	DOS 2.0

NLSFUNC	"National Language Support FUNCtion"	External	DOS 3.3
PATH	"PATH"	Internal	DOS 2.0
PRINT	"PRINT"	External	DOS 2.0
PROMPT	"PROMPT"	Internal	DOS 2.0
QBASIC	"Quick BASIC"	External	DOS 5.0
RECOVER	"RECOVER"	External	DOS 2.0
RMDIR	"ReMove DIRectory"	Internal	DOS 2.0
RD	"Remove Directory"	Internal	DOS 2.0
REN	"RENAme"	Internal	DOS 1.0
RENAME	"RENAME"	Internal	DOS 1.0
REPLACE	"REPLACE"	External	DOS 3.2
RESTORE	"RESTORE"	External	DOS 2.0
SELECT	"SELECT"	External	PC 1.0 / MS 3.3
SET	"SET"	Internal	DOS 2.0
SETUP	"SETUP"	External	DOS 5.0
SETVER	"SET VERsion"	External	DOS 5.0
SHARE	"SHARE"	External	DOS 3.0
SORT	"SORT"	External	DOS 2.0
SUBST	"SUBSTitute"	External	DOS 3.1
SYS	"SYStem"	External	DOS 1.0
TIME	"TIME"	Internal	DOS 1.0
TREE	"TREE"	External	DOS 3.2
TYPE	"TYPE"	Internal	DOS 1.0
UNDELETE	"UNDELETE"	External	DOS 5.0
UNFORMAT	"UNFORMAT"	External	DOS 5.0
VERIFY	"VERIFY"	Internal	DOS 2.0
VER	"VERsion"	Internal	DOS 2.0
VOL	"VOLume"	Internal	DOS 2.0
XCOPY	"eXtended COPY"	External	DOS 3.2

B: Batch File Commands and Variables

Batch file variables come in three types

- *Parameter variables* are indicated by a %, followed by a single digit (**0-9**).

  For example, with a batch file called **MYSORT.BAT**, entering this: **MYSORT Calif A:\SALES TEMP.TXT** would fill up four parameter variables used by the batch file:

%0	**MYSORT**	keyword
%1	**Calif**	the word you're sorting the file by
%2	**A:\SALES**	the file you're sorting
%3	**TEMP.TXT**	a temporary file to hold the output

- *Internal loop variables* are indicated by **%%**, followed by a character (e.g. **%%F**). These are used in **FOR** loops.

- *Named DOS environment variables* are variables previously declared in a **SET** command and can be used in a batch file if they are enclosed in % % (e.g. **%PATH%**).

Batch file commands are DOS commands intended specifically for batch files (though keywords and other DOS commands can also be used in batch files). A batch file must be an **ASCII** text file with the filename extension **.BAT**. The batch file commands:

CALL   Calls another batch file (available only in versions 3.3 and later).   Example: **CALL KEYWORD**

ECHO   Effects how messages and commands are displayed on the video screen.

Examples:

@ECHO OFF turns echo off so that the DOS prompt, commands, and **REM**arks are not displayed. The **@**, available only in versions 3.3 and greater, prevents the **ECHO OFF** command itself from being displayed.

ECHO ON turns the feature back on.

ECHO Message displays **Message** on the video regardless of whether **ECHO** is **ON** or **OFF**.

FOR   Also called **FOR/IN/DO**. Repeats commands in a loop.

Example: **FOR %%F IN (*.*) DO TYPE %%F**
This **TYPE**s each file in ***.*** sequentially.

GOTO   Jumps to another part of the batch file. Example:

```
@ECHO OFF
GOTO JUMP
REM This is skipped.
:JUMP
REM This is executed.
```

The **:** before **JUMP** makes it a label (a *target*) of the **GOTO**.

IF   Performs commands based on certain conditions. It has three different forms.

- Test for the existence of files. Example:

```
IF EXIST FILENAME.TXT GOTO PART2
   ...
:PART2
```

  If **FILENAME.TXT** exists, the execution skips over any other commands to **PART2** and proceeds from there. Note that **IF NOT EXIST** ... can also be used; it works similarly.

- Test variables. Examples:

```
IF %1==*.* ECHO True
IF NOT %1==*.* ECHO False
```

- Test for errors. Many programs return a DOS error code when they complete. Example:

```
IF ERRORLEVEL 1 ECHO Program error!
```

PAUSE   Pauses the action and displays a message.

Example:

PAUSE Is printer on and ready?

REM   Stands for **REM**ark. If **ECHO** is **ON**, the remark is displayed; otherwise it isn't. **REM** is best used for messages for the programmer.

Example:

REM This begins phase 2 of the batch file.

SHIFT   Shifts the parameter variable values down one—so that more than nine parameters can be used.

Example: **SHIFT**

Results: The value in %0 is lost;
             the value in %1 is renamed %0;
             the value in %2 is renamed %1;
             the value in %3 is renamed %2;

             .

             .

             .

             the value in %9 is renamed %8;
             %9 becomes the next parameter.

C: PROMPT Codes

The **PROMPT** command customizes the DOS prompt. You can use ordinary text and/or any of the following codes:

$D	=	Current date
$_	=	Go to next line
$T	=	Current time
$V	=	The current DOS version
$N	=	The current disk drive
$$	=	$
$P	=	The current path
$H	=	Backspace
$E	=	ESCape
$G	=	>
$L	=	<
$B	=	¦
$Q	=	=

Examples:

What you type	*What you may see*
PROMPT DOS$g	DOS>
PROMPT NG	A>
PROMPT PG	A:/>
PROMPT THHHHHHG	12:03>
PROMPT Yes, Dave?	Yes, Dave?
PROMPT	A>

D: Common Error Messages

Access denied. The read-only bit of a file is set.

Bad command or filename. You probably have a typo in the command. Or, the default path is probably not what you think it is.

Disk error ... Abort, Ignore, Retry, Fail? You probably forgot to put a disk into the disk drive.

File creation error. Either there was not enough room on the disk for a file or you tried to copy to a read-only file.

File not found. Either no files are in the specified directory, or else no file matches the wildcard you specified.

General failure. *Removable disk:* The disk is probably not formatted. *Fixed disk:* You're in deep sewage (you *did* back up your data files, didn't you?). You've probably had a read/write head crash into your disk; you'll have to go to a professional for help.

Incorrect DOS version. Only one version of DOS can be used at a time. If you boot with one version of DOS and then try to invoke a command of another version, you'll get this error message.

Insert COMMAND.COM disk in default drive and strike any key when ready. The last program overwrote **COMMAND.COM** in the computer's memory. You must reload **COMMAND.COM** before you can continue.

Insufficient memory. Your computer doesn't have enough memory to carry out a command.

Invalid drive specification. You probably made a typo when entering the disk drive.

Invalid parameter. You entered a parameter incorrectly.

Invalid path. The path you specified may not exist—or the default path is probably not what you think it is.

Non-system disk or disk error, replace and strike any key when ready. DOS needs the system files (**IO.SYS** and **MSDOS.SYS**). Put a bootable disk into the default drive.

Sector not found. The disk has one or more defective sectors. See "**General failure.**"

Specified drive does not exist or is non-removable. You probably tried to invoke **DISKCOMP** or **DISKCOPY** on a fixed disk. This isn't allowed.

Too many files open. DOS doesn't have enough "handles" for the number of files your program wants to open at once. Cure: Increase the number of **FILES** allowed (i.e. change the **FILES=** statement in the **CONFIG.SYS** file).

Write protect error. You tried to write to a disk which has the write protect notch covered.

E: Using Alternative Characters

Here are the alternative characters and their ASCII decimal values:

Value	Char.	Value	Char.	Value	Char.	Value	Char.
128	Ç	160	á	192	└	224	α
129	ü	161	í	193	┴	225	β
130	é	162	ó	194	┬	226	Γ
131	â	163	ú	195	├	227	Π
132	ä	164	ñ	196	─	228	Σ
133	à	165	Ñ	197	┼	229	σ
134	å	166	ª	198	╞	230	μ
135	ç	167	º	199	╟	231	γ
136	ê	168	¿	200	╚	232	Φ
137	ë	169	⌐	201	╔	233	θ
138	è	170	¬	202	╩	234	Ω
139	ï	171	½	203	╦	235	δ
140	î	172	¼	204	╠	236	ω
141	ì	173	¡	205	═	237	φ
142	Ä	174	«	206	╬	238	ε
143	Å	175	»	207	╧	239	η
144	É	176	▓	208	╨	240	Ξ
145	æ	177	▒	209	╤	241	±
146	Æ	178	▓	210	╥	242	≥
147	ô	179	│	211	╙	243	≤
148	ö	180	┤	212	╘	244	⌠
149	ò	181	╡	213	╒	245	⌡
150	û	182	╢	214	╓	246	÷
151	ù	183	╖	215	╫	247	≈
152	ÿ	184	╕	216	╪	248	°
153	Ö	185	╣	217	┘	249	·
154	Ü	186	║	218	┌	250	·
155	¢	187	╗	219	█	251	√
156	£	188	╝	220	▄	252	ⁿ
157	¥	189	╜	221	▌	253	²
158	₧	190	╛	222	▐	254	■
159	ƒ	191	┐	223	▀	255	

Using alternative characters with DOS can be very easy—or not.

Problem: How can you display the ä character? There are no keys on the keyboard to do this.

Solution: Hold down the **ALT** key while typing the three-digit ASCII value (132). Then release the **ALT** key.

That method is fine if you use alternative characters only occasionally. But what if you want to touch-type in another language? You can use DOS to change the layout of your keyboard, but there are many roadblocks in the way:

- You must prepare the **CONFIG.SYS** and **AUTOEXEC.BAT** files and reboot the computer—no big deal unless you have to do it several times to get things to come out right.

- You may change the ASCII code (the DOS manuals call this "changing the code page"). Unless you know the new codes, you'll have difficulties. Your particular hardware may not support the code pages you need, so you may get cryptic error messages and not know if the problem is the hardware or something else.

- Different versions of DOS handle international support in various ways. The commands are different—and the same commands are even entered differently—so beware!

If you do choose to change your keyboard's layout, your DOS manuals are *essential*. Study them carefully before beginning!

F: Using the DOS Shell—Versions 4.0 and 4.01*

What Good Is It?

You've already read a little bit about shells—what they are and why they were created (see pages 116-118 for a refresher).

As you know, the DOS Shell is a *second-level* shell. It puts a second layer of interpretive "friendliness" between you and the kernel operating system program, **MSDOS.SYS**. Remember that the first layer of shell is the **COMMAND.COM** command interpreter program, which offers you the DOS prompt.

The DOS Shell's main contribution to friendliness is the set of menus it offers. You select items from the menu rather than type in commands. Also, the *Shell* has these other advantages:

- Its windows present a lot of information more *visually*—including the files you want to view.

- Its menus can be customized—even with passwords—to start programs. By customizing the menus, you can depart from the strict tree structure of a disk. The tree is still on the disk, but the menus can organize programs differently.

- It lets you use a mouse.

---

*The Shell for DOS 5 is covered in chapter 11 (pages 218-243). Since this (DOS 4) Shell is not practical for removable disks, the examples in this appendix are only for computers with fixed disks. If you have only removable disks, you might want to read along here—to see what you're missing!—but don't bother to do the examples.

Learning the Basics

Enough talk. You need some hands on experience with the Shell. How do you get started? You install the Shell with the DOS *Install* disk. Hopefully, you did this when you ran the *Install* disk, but if not, you're not too late....

Do It Now: Place the *Install* disk into the **A:** drive and boot your computer (even if you have files on a fixed disk, you can install DOS again. The fixed disk will not be reformatted and your files will not be lost). Follow the directions on the screen carefully; be sure to answer yes when asked if you want to install the DOS Shell.

Make sure the **PRINT** command is installed. If you are in the DOS Shell, press F3 to exit. Then, from the DOS prompt, enter **PRINT**. If the message says, **Name of list device [PRN]**, just press ←ENTER to install **PRINT**. If the message says **PRINT queue is empty**, then **PRINT** is already installed.

Now you can get to the Shell in one of two ways:

- When you boot your computer, DOS may automatically put you in the Shell;

- At the DOS prompt, enter **DOSSHELL**.

Choose one of these ways now, and go into the DOS Shell....

Selecting vs. Typing

A big problem with the DOS prompt is that you must memorize the commands and type them in—so if you don't know what the commands are, you can't use them (which can be totally exasperating)!

The alternative is to *select* commands from a *menu*. The DOS Shell gives you various ways to do this—one with a mouse; one without.

With a **mouse**, you select an item on the screen by "pointing" to it and clicking a button on the mouse.*

Without a mouse, you use *keys*—F10, TAB, and the arrow keys—to highlight items on the screen (then ←ENTER to make the actual selection). While some people prefer this method so they don't have to take their hands off the keyboard, this makes screen cursor movement slower, and more confusing and frustrating. So without a mouse, the Shell is often more trouble than convenience.

Of course, the mouse doesn't have to select everything. Some of the Shell's features *are* selected more easily with function keys.

The first of these, F1, *helps* you with the rest of the Shell....

---

*If your mouse has two or more buttons, you'll use one of them—the left-hand button—almost exclusively.

Help Windows

Get Help: _Select_ (using mouse or keyboard) the **F1=Help** in the upper right-hand corner of the screen or press F1.

The Help system is _context sensitive._ That is, the Shell makes a good guess as to the problem you're having and brings up the (hopefully) right window of advice for you to read. If it's not the right window, you can also get an _index_ of all the Help windows available....

Try It: Using either mouse or keyboard, select the word **Index** in the first Help window. If you have an F11 key, it may get the index.   Otherwise, press **ALT F1** (simultaneously).* You have 75 Help windows, including two special types:

- _Help on Help:_ Press F1 from _within_ a Help window, to see another window that "helps you with Help."

- _Help with Keys:_ Press F9 from _within_ a Help window to get a special Help window which explains the many ways to use certain keys on the keyboard.

When you've finished with Help, press the ESC key to return to what you were doing before.

---

*This combination isn't shown anywhere on the screen; you simply need to remember it.

Starting Programs

Notice the **_Main menu_** of the DOS Shell—where you can select programs to start. The good news is: You can add any program you want
to this menu list; thereafter, _you start that program simply by selecting
its menu item._

OK: Can you put the **EDLIN** text editor program onto this menu?

Yep: _Step 1_—tell DOS that you want to add something to the menu:
Select the **Program** item on the second line of the display, and
see the following choices:

> **Start**   Starts the program highlighted in the menu.
> **Add**   Adds a program title to the menu.
> **Change**   Changes a program title.
> **Delete**   Deletes a program title from the menu.
> **Copy**   Copies a program title from one group to another.

Step 2—select **Add** from the above choices.

Step 3:—give the program title: The first box on the resulting
screen is **Title**, which lets you specify the item's appearance
in the menu. Enter **EDLIN: The DOS Line Editor**.

So far, so good—but that's just the title—the menu item's
appearance in the menu. You still need to tell the Shell what
to do when that item is actually selected....

Step 4—enter the commands: Press TAB to move the cursor to the second box (**Commands**). Here you tell the Shell how to start the program, by entering these commands. Press:

C: F4 CD \DOS F4 EDLIN [ ] F4 PAUSE

Notice that you press F4 to signal the end of each of these commands:

Change the disk drive:	**C:**
Change the directory:	**CD \DOS**
Start the program:	**EDLIN [ ]**
One more instruction:	**PAUSE**

EDLIN, as you know, must have a filename as a parameter, so the **[ ]** tells the DOS Shell that when **EDLIN** is selected as a menu item, the Shell *must ask you* for this parameter.

The **PAUSE** instruction simply tells DOS to wait for you to finish reading the screen before returning to the Shell.

Step 5—enter the Help text (press TAB to get to the third dialog box): Here you can write the help message *you* would want to see if you need help with **EDLIN**. Type whatever you want:

This is your help text, etc., etc.

Step 6—enter a password (press TAB one more time, to get to the fourth dialog box): Enter **EC** (for Easy Course). That's now the password for using **EDLIN**.

Step 7—end the procedure: Press F2 (or point to and click on **Save**).... The new item appears in the menu!

Does your new menu item work as you intended?

Test It: First, test the customized Help window.

Like So: Highlight your item, **EDLIN: The DOS Line Editor** in the menu (with a mouse, just point and click). Now press [F1] and your customized Help window will appear.... Read at your leisure, then press [ESC] to get rid of the Help window.

Next: Test the password.

Do It: Try starting **EDLIN: The DOS Line Editor** (with a mouse, you double-click—two rapid clicks in succession). A window will appear, *requesting the password.* Enter **EC**.

Then: Tell the Shell what file to edit with **EDLIN**.

Do It: A window asks you to **Type the parameters**. So (with your *Power* disk in the **A:** drive) enter the filename in the box provided: **A:\WORD\PEOPLE\TODO.TXT**

As soon as you do this, the Shell disappears and the **EDLIN** program starts (you'll see **EDLIN**'s distinctive ***** prompt). So do something, say, enter **L** to List the **TODO.TXT** file— just to prove that you're editing the right file. Then enter **E** to Exit **EDLIN** and return to the Shell.

Groups

Group in the DOS Shell is just another word for *menu*.

The Shell initially has two groups: The **Main** group (Main menu), and the **DOS Utilities** group—a sub-group, since you get to it by selecting an item from the **Main** group. You can tell when a menu item—such as **DOS Utilities...**—does indeed lead to a sub-group (menu) because it's followed by **....**

To see how a group (menu) works, select (double-click on) **DOS Utilities....** You'll get another menu, which consists of DOS commands. Press ESC to return to the Main group (menu).

Challenge: Can you copy the **EDLIN** menu item from the **Main** group to the **DOS Utilities** group?

No Sweat: Highlight **EDLIN: The DOS Line Editor**
(that's a single click with the mouse)
Select **Program**
Select **Copy** (instructions will appear on the screen)*
Select **DOS Utilities...** (double-click)
Press F2

The **EDLIN** menu item is now copied to the **DOS Utilities** group.

---

*Remember, the password is **EC**.

Issuing Commands

You can give some commands to DOS via the Shell.

You're already in the right place to do it—just look at the menu items in the `DOS Utilities...` group ...

> `Set Date and Time`
> `Disk Copy`
> `Disk Compare`
> `Backup fixed disk`
> `Restore fixed disk`
> `Format`

Looks familiar, eh? These are just the same old commands you've been reading about—and typing from the DOS prompt. Select one and you'll get a window asking the parameters needed to carry out the command.

Ho Hum: Make a current copy of the _Power_ disk to the _Power Backup_ disk..

Nothin' To It: Select `Disk Copy`.
Change the parameters, if necessary.
Follow the instructions on the screen.

From the `DOS Utilities` menu, press ESC to return to the `Main` menu.

Using the File System

The DOS Shell File System is your Shell's executive secretary. It does just about everything for you—except maybe bring you coffee.

So, where is the File System?

Right Here: From the main menu of the DOS Shell, simply select File System and you'll go right to it (do this now).

Exactly what you see now depends on your particular computer system (so leave that issue for a moment). For starters, put the *Power* disk into the **A:** drive and select the **A** in the upper left corner of the screen.

Now, just as cream and sugar make coffee taste better, so the File System helps the palatability of DOS.* It divides the screen into two displays....

The Cream: The Directory Tree, on the left, shows the tree of the currently selected disk—the *Power* disk.

The Sugar: There's a *list of files* on the right (right now it's just a message: **No files in selected directory**).

---

*Of course, some people like their coffee black; they prefer the DOS prompt to the DOS Shell.

Question: Why don't you see a list of files?

Answer: Because the root directory of the *Power* disk doesn't contain any files right now.

All Right: How can you see a list of the files in the DOS directory of the *Power* disk?

Like So: Just select the word **DOS** in the disk tree (if you have a mouse, point and click at **DOS**; otherwise, [TAB] until one of the directories is highlighted, then use the arrow keys to highlight DOS, and press [←ENTER]).... What you see on the right half of your screen is a list of the files in the DOS directory of your *Power* disk (those are the DOS commands you've copied there throughout this book). Notice that these files are in alphabetical order!

And Look: Select other directories from the disk tree on the left side of the screen. In each case, you'll see an alphabetical listing of that directory's files on the right half of the screen. To get files and directories from another disk, just select **A**, **B**, **C**, etc., from the disk drive icons in the upper left part of the screen.

The cream and sugar of the File System—the tree listing and the file list—are great even when used separately. But when you combine them, you *really* get a lot of power....

Take a closer look at the file list. Each line shows the following:

- An icon—the little picture of a file folder at the left—which highlights when the file is selected;

- The size of the file, in bytes;

- The date when the file was last changed.

Also, notice the **✱.✱** at the top of the list. As you remember from pages 170-174, this wildcard means "all files in the selected directory." So that's what the file list is currently displaying.

Then, at the right of the file list is a **scroll bar** (with arrows at top and bottom), which you can use to move through the files on the screen. That's right—*unlike* the regular **DIR**ectory command (which gives you only one chance to read)—you can easily scroll up and down the file list like this, scanning the entire list back and forth.

Look Around: Can you use the File System quickly and easily to flip through the files on your fixed disk?

Piece of Cake: Select the **C** icon to show the tree for your fixed disk. Then select any directory from the tree and get a list of its files on the right side of the screen. Use the scroll bars to move your disk tree and your file lists up and down....

Beats the heck out of the DOS prompt, doesn't it?

Doing Things to Files

Of course, you don't just *look* at files, you *do* things with them....

Get Ready: Make sure the *Power* disk is in the **A :** drive. Select the **A** icon so that the tree for the *Power* disk is displayed. Then select the **\DOS** directory.

Get Set: Before you can do something with a file, you have to select one. So, select the **CHKDSK** file: Point and click at the **CHKDSK** file with a mouse; or TAB and use the arrow keys to highlight **CHKDSK** and finally press the space bar.

Note the visual difference here between *highlighting* a file and *selecting* it: When a file is selected, the small icon next to the filename is highlighted as well as the filename itself. *And you can select more than one file at once.* Then, once you've selected the file(s) you can start doing things....

Go: Start **CHKDSK** from the File System. Select **File** from the upper left corner of the screen. A ***drop-down menu*** appears. Select **Open (Start)** and a window will ask for options. Enter **/V** for the Verbose switch The Shell disappears and the command, **CHKDSK /V**, is performed. Then the Shell returns.

Practice using the File System now, with these tasks....

Task: Print the **SHOP.TXT** file (be sure the printer is on and ready): Select the **\WORD\PEOPLE** directory, then the **SHOP.TXT** file. Select **File** and then **Print**.... Voilá!

Next: Set up the text files so that you can open them with **EDLIN** directly from the File System: Select the **\EDITLINE** directory, then **EDLIN**. Select **File** and **Associate**. At the window, enter **TXT**. This *associates* all **.TXT** files with the **EDLIN** command. Press (←ENTER), then select **Do not prompt**.

So now test this new association: Select the **\WORD\PEOPLE** directory, then **ADDRESS.TXT**. Select **File** and **Open (Start)**.... **See?** DOS leaves the Shell and runs **EDLIN**, after loading the **ADDRESS.TXT** file. Enter **L**, for List, to see the **ADDRESS.TXT** file. Enter **E**, for Exit, to leave **EDLIN**. **DOS** will return you to the Shell.

Then: Move **EDLIN** from the **\EDITLINE** directory to the **\DOS** directory. Select the **\EDITLINE** directory, then **EDLIN**. Select **File** and **Move**. A dialog window will ask for the destination, so then enter **A:\DOS**. The file is then moved to **\DOS** and erased from **\EDITLINE**—all in one step!

Now: Copy **EDLIN** back to the **\EDITLINE** directory. Select the **\DOS** directory, then select **EDLIN**. Select **File** and **Copy**. A dialog window will ask for the destination, so then enter **A:\EDITLINE**. The file is *copied* to **\EDITLINE**; it also remains in **\DOS**.

Now: Delete **EDLIN** in the **\EDITLINE** directory: First, select the **\EDITLINE** directory, then the **EDLIN** file. Then select **File** and **Delete**. You will be asked (twice) to confirm that you really do want to delete the file.

And: Rename the **MEMO.TXT** file to **MEMO2.TXT**: Select the **\WORD\PEOPLE** directory, then the **MEMO.TXT** file. Select **File** and **Rename**. Enter **MEMO2.TXT**; now that's the name.

Then: Make **SHOP.TXT** a *hidden file*: Select **SHOP.TXT**, then **File** and **Change attribute**. In the first dialog window, choose to change files one at a time. In the next window, highlight **Hidden**, press the space bar and select **Enter** (or press ⟨←ENTER⟩). **SHOP.TXT** is now a hidden file; it will not appear in all **DIR**ectory listings.

Last: Add a **BOB** directory to **\WORD\PEOPLE**: Select **File** and **Create directory**. Then, in the dialog box, enter **BOB**.

By now, you should be starting to "get the hang" of the Shell's menu-oriented way of managing your files. It's just a matter of selecting the file(s) you want to adjust, and then selecting the things you want to do.

Of course, the Shell can't do everything—but the things it *does* do are as easy as pointing and clicking with a mouse. And there's more....

Options: How Much Help Do You Want?

For more power and convenience in handling files, you have certain _options_ you can set in the Shell. These options affect the way that files are displayed and handled in the File System.

Example: Display the **\WORD\PEOPLE** directory so that only **.TXT** (not **.BAK**) files are displayed—by order of their dates.

Like This: Select **Options** and **Display Options**. In the dialog box, type ***.TXT** (do not press ←ENTER yet) to indicate that you want all **.TXT** files. Then select **Date** (just press TAB if you don't have a mouse). _Now_ press or select ←ENTER.... Voilá!

Now you don't need to clutter up the screen and your eyes—with the redundancy of all the backup files.

Good Practice: Return to the standard display.
Select **Options** and **Display Options**.
Type ***.***; and select **Name**. This will display all files in alphabetical order, as before.

You can make your own safety net with the File System by having DOS double check with you before erasing or overwriting files. Just ...

Try It: Select **Options** and **File Options**

Select **Confirm on delete**

Select **Confirm on replace***

Recommendation: Leave **Select across directories** turned off (i.e. do *not* select it).

Normally, you can select only among files listed in the current directory; **Select across directories** allows you to select files from different directories, at once. *However,* you may forget which files in other directories are selected, thus accidentally doing things to unknown files—so do yourself a favor and leave this option alone.

Do you see how the File System's **Options** can help you do your file management work more efficiently?

And there's one more powerful option you ought to know....

---

*Recommendation: If you're going to move many files from one directory to another, temporarily turn off the **Confirm on replace** option. Otherwise, you'll be asked to individually confirm file after file, ad nauseam.

Arrange: The Big Picture

The **Arrange** option is the best cure for Murphy's Tree Law: "No matter where you put a file, you'll later look for it in another directory."

Quick: What directory on your _Power_ disk has the **COPY.TXT** file?

"Uh..." Who knows? It simply isn't possible to remember the exact locations of all your many files. That's why the **Arrange** option is handy: Select **Arrange**, then **System file list**, then **COPY.TXT**. Now all files on the _Power_ disk are listed alphabetically, regardless of their directories.

Notice, too, the information displayed about the **COPY.TXT** file—its directory, its attribute bits, etc. And to see what's in that file, just select **File** and **View** (recall that you made **COPY.TXT** on page 168—to practice with **COPY**).

Press (ESC) to stop viewing and return to the File System.

Also, **Arrange** has two other options besides **System file list**:

- **Single file list**—the standard file list which you saw first.

- **Multiple file list**—shows the files from two directories at once—one above the other—to let you compare the files.

Now select **Single file list**, to go back to where you were.

Shell Game

1. Does the DOS Shell replace the DOS prompt?

2. Can you use the DOS Shell without a mouse?

3. How do you: Start the DOS Shell from the DOS prompt? Find a particular Help screen? Initiate any DOS command in the **DOS Utilities** group?

4. Put **CHKDSK** as an item on the **Main** menu of the DOS Shell. Give it the title **CHKDSK: The DOS Check Disk Command**. Then give it this Help message: **Checks a disk**. Use the password **EC2**, and have the display pause before returning to the Shell. Next, test all aspects of this entry. Finally, copy this new menu item into the **DOS Utilities** group.

5. What's the largest file (in bytes) on the *Power* disk?

6. How can you find all of the **JOHN.TXT** files on the *Power* disk?

7. You **View** a text file; you **Open** a text file. What's the difference?

Watch the Pea

1. The DOS prompt requires you to type in commands; the Shell offers menu items to be selected. But when you execute a DOS command from the Shell, **COMMAND.COM** is still called to do the work. So the DOS Shell *enhances* **COMMAND.COM**—by helping to interpret it—but it does *not* replace it; the Shell does many things well, but it won't do everything the prompt does.

2. It's possible—but not worth the trouble: You use a combination of F10, TAB, and the arrow keys to move around. Phooey.

3. First, the DOS Shell must be installed using the DOS *Install* disk. Once that's done, you can get to the Shell from the DOS prompt by entering **DOSSHELL**.

   To find any particular Help screen in the Shell, press F1 for help; then press F11 or ALT F1 to get an index of Help screens. Then you can select the particular Help screen you want.

   To initiate a command from the **DOS Utilities** group, start a command just as you start a program—double-click it.

4. Select **Program** and **Add**. In the first dialog box, type:
   CHKDSK: The DOS Check Disk Command

   (TAB) to the second dialog box—here's the tough one. Type this:
   C: (F4) **CD \DOS** (F4) **CHKDSK C:** (F4) **PAUSE**

   Remember that the (F4) is the keystroke you use to separate commands in a multi-part command line such as this.

C:	is the disk drive location of **CHKDSK**.
CD \DOS	changes the directory to **\DOS**
CHKDSK C:	gives the command itself.
PAUSE	pauses the display before going to the Shell.

   Now (TAB) to the third dialog box. Enter your Help text: **Checks a disk**.

   (TAB) to the password box and enter **EC2**—the password. Then, to save all of this, press (F2). The new item is now in the **Main** menu.

   To test this new item, select **CHKDSK: The DOS Check Disk Command** from the Main menu (with a mouse, just double-click on it). When asked for the password, enter **EC2**. The shell disappears and **CHKDSK** takes over.... After **CHKDSK** finishes, just press any key to return to the Shell. Then, to test the help screen, highlight **CHKDSK: The DOS Check Disk Command** (single click) and press (F1). Your customized Help window appears.

   To move the **CHKDSK** menu item, first highlight it. Then select **Program** and **Copy**. Enter the **EC2** password. Then select **DOS Utilities...** (double-click). Press (F2).

5. To find out, select the **File System** from the **Main** menu. Select the **A** disk drive, then **Options**, **Display Options**, and **Size**. This lists the files by their sizes. Now select **Arrange** and **System file list**. This includes all of the files on the disk—so all of the files on the **A:** drive are now displayed by order of size. The largest one is displayed first— **REPLACE** is largest.

6. Select **Options** and **Display Options**. In the dialog box, enter **JOHN*.TXT**. Now, only **JOHN** text files are displayed. Highlight various ones among these, and you'll see that they're in various directories—because the **JOHN** files were guinea pigs when you practiced other DOS commands.

7. When you **View** a text file, you stay in the Shell's File System; no other program is involved, and no setup is needed. And of course, no changes can be made to the file.

   When you **Open** a text file, you actually exit the File System and enter another program—say, **EDLIN** or another word processor. Then, of course, the file can be changed. Remember that to do this kind of file opening from the File System, you must first set up the File System with **File** and **Associate**.

Index

References do not include every usage but refer to major explanations. For a list of all DOS-prompt commands, see pages 76 and 325-327.

Reader Comments

We here at Grapevine love to hear feedback about our publications. It helps us produce books tailored to our readers' needs. If you have any specific comments or advice for our authors after reading this book, we'd appreciate hearing from you!

Which of our books do you have?

Comments, Advice and Suggestions:

May we use your comments as testimonials?

Your Name: Profession:

City, State:

How long have you had your computer?

Please send Grapevine catalogs to the following persons:

Name _____

Address _____

City _____ State _____ Zip _____

Name _____

Address _____

City _____ State _____ Zip _____

By the way, if you liked this book, there are many others that you—or someone you know—will certainly enjoy also. Here are descriptions of a couple of them:

An Easy Course in Using WordPerfect

This friendly, well-paced tutorial uses a learn-by-doing approach to bring you to comfort and proficiency with WordPerfect (versions 5.0 and 5.1), from the basics of editing and formatting to the intricacies of tables, indexes, and mail-merge. The example-rich, chapter-by-chapter format offers quizzes and notes at regular intervals. *Easy Courses* feel like real, live classrooms. They <u>teach</u> —with energy and patience.

A Little DOS Will Do You

Here's a fast, easy way to get up-to-speed on just the bare basics of DOS—the heart of your IBM or IBM-compatible personal computer. This short, little book covers version 4.01 and any earlier versions of DOS, giving you quick, hands-on lessons on disks, directories, shells, files, pathnames, menus and more. As you progress through the lessons, you'll build and modify your own files and directories.

For more details on these books or any of our titles, <u>check with your local bookseller or calculator/computer dealer</u>.

For a full Grapevine catalog, write, call or fax:

Grapevine Publications, Inc.
626 N.W. 4th Street   P.O. Box 2449
Corvallis, Oregon 97339-2449 U.S.A.
Phone: 1-800-338-4331 *or* 503-754-0583
Fax: 503-754-6508